Signs, Songs and Stories

another look at children's liturgies

Virginia Sloyan

Editor

The Liturgical Conference

Washington, D.C.

Virginia Sloyan is program assistant of the Senior Center Humanities Program at The National Council on the Aging, Washington, D.C.

The editor wishes to thank Melissa Kay Wood for her editorial consultation; Kay Kircher for the cover design; John Henry for layout design; Daniel Shames for layout; Sister Angela Herbert, R.S.M. and Tom Korkames for help in the preparation of the book; the authors; and the entire staff of the Liturgical Conference.

Photographs are by Gene Yagow (pp. 5, 14, 27, 28, 61); Geroge R. Cassidy (20, 24); George Koshollek (9, 42); Ray Barth (11); Richard T. Lee (36); Bob Workman (47); Frank Methe (54); Mr. Lorsung (59); and John Henry.

Second printing, March 1975. Third printing, October 1982 by The Liturgical Press (cover design for third printing by Ann Blattner). ISBN 0-8146-1285-7

CONTENTS

Where Are We Going?

another look at children's liturgies

Children's liturgies. A phrase that was non-existent in the vocabulary of Christians as recently as ten years ago has, in that short time span, found its place not only in speech patterns but, more significantly, among things to be "concerned about." Concern always generates activity. And the activity in this area today can be described as nothing short of phenomenal.

It is not in the least surprising that an intensity of interest in children's worship, on the part of Christian parents, religious educators and priests, has emerged in recent years. In fact, given the Roman church's history of almost total concentration on children as the fitting objects of religious endeavor (instructional and experiential), it is a quite natural development here, at least, that a new found interest in liturgical celebration would carry over into children's programs.

Interest in the worship patterns of children is one thing; preoccupation is another. It would be an unfortunate development—and signs of this trend are already in our midst—if a disproportionate amount of energy, time and effort were devoted to the worship needs of the young, with the quite natural consequence of neglecting, or giving diminished attention to, the worship needs of the whole Christian community.

The forces of history and custom are not solely responsible for the existing tendency, in some parochial settings, toward heightened activity in the realm of children's liturgies, at the expense of liturgical activity that is more universal in nature. There are other factors, among them: (1) Our present parochial structures, by and large, continue to work assiduously at the creation and perpetuation of communities of children. The next focus of activity is the teen-ager. Adults in the parish are "reached" (that is usually the word used, and rather accurate in view of the approach involved) most often through their children. On occasion, this process does, in fact, work toward the creation of family communities within a parish, some of which survive beyond the immediate situations which have brought them into existence—e.g., preparation for infant baptism, for first communion, confirmation, etc. Only on

1

rare occasion does the process serve the larger need of creating a total faith community. (2) There is a common misconception that planning liturgies for children, or for children and their parents, makes fewer and less rigorous demands—in the realm of study—than planning for the larger community. Hard work is not the commodity that is feared and thus avoided—quite the contrary, in fact. Rather, what is too often avoided is the effort of learning what liturgy *is* and what it *is not*; grasping the basic principles of good liturgical celebration; and lastly, taking the time to study the Bible. (3) Laypersons and clergy alike, suffering under parochial or diocesan restrictions in the area of liturgical celebration, find that they are freer to create good liturgies if the focus of their activity is the young.

SUBCULTURE OR FAITH COMMUNITY?

In the face of these and other considerations, it seems valid enough to suggest that a subculture of children's liturgies is fairly firmly established in parishes throughout the country, and promises to enjoy a lively future. Persons who see only good in such a development rationalize their optimism in these, or similar, phrases: "Well, *at least* the children in our parish are involved in liturgy. They love to come to church." "At some of our family masses, we see adults involved in celebration for the first time in their lives." And the final, "Besides, good children's masses can't help but lead to efforts in a broader direction. The people will be demanding good liturgy at the other parish masses."

The author of these lines has serious difficulty subscribing to this line of reasoning. To hold that the formation of a faith community is brought about, directly or indirectly, through efforts channeled primarily toward children and adolescents, is, I believe, a conviction bordering on the absurd. Are we willing to look realistically at the results of the catechetical endeavors of the last forty years, and then conclude that yes, this is the way that Christians, and Christian communities, are formed? To work tirelessly, and exclusively, on the formation of the young—through liturgy, through catechetics (and all the experiences that these words suggest)—with the dream that *things will be different when they are the adults of our parishes*, its leaders and its ministers, is to misread the normal patterns of human behavior.

Communities of faith shared . . . that is what the church is about, and has always been about. The formation of such communities *now*—not ten years from now, or twenty—is our mandate as Christians. " . . . the Church is not for the liturgy, nor the liturgy for the Church," Aidan Kavanagh reminds us, "but the liturgy *is* the Church *enacting itself* under the sole criteria of the gospel in a given place and time. The Church is a community of faith shared that liturgically actualizes, by celebrating, its collective communion in the gospel of Jesus Christ, in whom alone life in all its fullness is to be found."

Father Kavanagh goes on to make a point that is very significant for all who are engaged in the work of liturgy planning—whether it be for adults or children: " . . . mere reform of the liturgy takes second place at best to renewal of the communion that is Christian life. To a people who know little or nothing about what such a communion, or a life lived together in faith, entails—having rarely if ever lived it—the liturgy will be not only an ineffective 'teacher' but an actual enhancer of the problem itself . . . The liturgy is not the malaise in this situation, the Church itself is. Adding audiovisual effects, banners, and contemporary music to such a liturgy is to put Band-Aids on cancer . . . " ("Teaching Through the Liturgy," *Notre Dame Journal of Education*, Spring 1974, Vol. 5, No. 1, pp. 35-47.)

The ways that such a communion, or "life lived together in faith," is formed, nourished, sustained, while not the thrust of this particular chapter, must be the primary concern of all who would center their lives on the gospel of Jesus Christ . . . and thus the primary concern of liturgy planners, whether the liturgy in question is the parish Sunday mass, the special family celebration for the Second Sunday of Advent, or the classroom festivity that marks the feast of St. Francis.

If a faith community *exists* in a parish, then there is something to enter, to become part of; now our particular work with children—specifically, helping them to learn what and how to celebrate in the Lord Jesus—makes some sense; the larger context within which our task is set lends validity to the whole venture. Now our efforts to create celebrations, on occasion, for other segments of the parish community—the old, the hard of hearing, the physically and mentally handicapped—celebrations especially adapted to their particular gifts and needs, all make sense. They are *always* part of a larger picture, and always take second place to the formation of the total parish community.

WHAT MAKES THE EUCHARIST SPECIAL?

This brings us to the next question: "Should there be special masses for children?" For some reason, it is this question which is raised immediately in any discussion of children's liturgies. Not only is it explored first, but its exploration often signals the end of the discussion, and the beginning of un-limited (and exclusive) activity in this direction. The question has been answered affirmatively by the majority of Christians concerned about such things. The recently issued Directory for Masses with Children from the Congregation for Divine Worship (November 1, 1973) has had the effect of stilling the fears of the more cautious, and virtually making the question a non-question.

It is raised here for the reason that a simple "yes" does not do justice to the larger question it poses, namely: Should the Sunday eucharist be tailored to fit the needs of various segments of the worshiping community? And if yes, should there not then be special (regular) Sunday eucharistic celebrations for the old, for the psychologically disturbed, for adults who are illiterate, for teen-agers, for the retarded, etc.? The eucharist, we maintain, is *the* sign of

3

unity of the worshiping community. That is what makes it special. It
envisions the oneness, and solidarity, of all creatures in Jesus Christ under the
dominion of the Father. Does it not seem paradoxical that massive efforts are
being exerted to "do something" to the eucharistic rite so that it can be
participated in more fully . . . now by one segment of the faith community,
now by another, and tomorrow by yet another? Would it not make eminently
more sense to look very closely, first, at the way our Sunday parish masses
are being celebrated, and ask ourselves the hard question: *"Why* the compelling
need to adapt to these several special groupings so that involvement on their
part is possible?" There is a very good chance that the highly verbal nature
of our Sunday eucharists precludes involvement not merely by children, not
merely by adults who are not word-oriented, but by *all* who are seeking a
genuine ritual expression for their faith in Jesus risen.

The Directory for Masses with Children has been hailed as a breakthrough of
quite significant proportion: *"Finally*, the worship needs of children have been
recognized and addressed by church authorities." It is surely a breakthrough,
and we can only be grateful for the creativity that it encourages. One hesitates
to sound a discordant note in a chorus of harmony and praise, but it seems
imperative to do so . . . or at least to suggest a few reservations. The
Directory does not address itself to the urgent need for planning eucharistic
celebrations which, through the richness of their variety (of gesture and
silence and touch and song and word), and the beauty of their simplicity, have
the potential to speak to and for the tremendously diverse needs of an average
community. It tacitly assumes that present liturgical practice *is* serving the
needs of adult Christians, and is not serving the needs of children. ("Although
the mother tongue may now be used at Mass, still the words and signs have
not been sufficiently adapted to the capacity of children.")

It singles out certain aspects of a celebration as being especially worthy of
attention when considering the needs of children. A few examples: "It is
the responsibility of the priest who celebrates with children to make the celebration festive, fraternal, meditative. Even more than in Masses with adults,
the priest should try to bring about this kind of spirit." "The principles of
active and conscious participation are in a sense even more valid for Masses
celebrated with children. Every effort should be made to increase this
participation and to make it more intense." "The development of gestures,
postures, and actions is very important for Masses with children in view of
the nature of liturgy as an activity of the entire man and in view of the
psychology of children."

One welcomes the "official" urgings toward warm presidential style, active
participation, the use of song and gesture and action in masses celebrated with
children, and cannot help but wonder, at the same time, why these elements
are considered to be more appropriate for children than adults.

Lastly, the very nature of the Directory—it is, after all, exclusively concerned
with masses for children—tends to imply that the primary focus of concern
and activity for those engaged in planning children's liturgies is the eucharist.

4

And this implication, we might suggest, is open to question. The readers of *Signs, Songs and Stories* are invited to explore this question, and others, very seriously. What will be perceived throughout the essays which follow is the general conviction that time and energies given to the planning and celebration of simple, non-eucharistic liturgies with and for children—in the setting of home, classroom and church (or church hall)—are well worth all the effort that they involve; that the enterprise should be seen in its proper perspective, i.e., as subsidiary to the task of helping the larger parish community to understand and live its baptismal commitment; that the practice of scheduling special "family" masses throughout the year—not with great frequency, but on occasion—should be encouraged; and that the great "hinges" of the liturgical year (as Ralph Keifer refers to them in his essay)—the First Sunday of Advent, Christmas, the First Sunday of Lent, Easter, Pentecost—are not occasions for segregating any one segment of the community for purposes of common worship, but for including and involving all.

BRINGING IT HOME

It is a fact that large numbers of Christian adults have become motivated to learn more about the baptismal faith that is theirs in order to pass it on to their children. Through the efforts of professional religious educators, many of these parents have come to the conclusion that they themselves are the most effective "educators" of their offspring in matters of faith. While heavy emphasis has been placed on imparting to these adults correct notions of what the eucharist is, what the other sacraments are, what the church is, what the moral imperatives of the gospel are, etc., much less emphasis has been put on ritual practices in the home. As a result, the faith tradition being conveyed, or shared, is characterized by a certain sterility. Its context, generally, is not one of prayer—prayer in the company of others, prayer in keeping with the rhythm of feasts and seasons, prayer expressed in song and blessings and body movement, prayer that uses symbols like water and bread and salt to say what words can't say. A faith tradition needs signs, strong signs, through which it can be expressed; without them it remains isolated from life, in spite of valiant attempts to relate it to the ordinary and the real.

Persons engaged in the work of planning celebrations for children in a parochial setting must view their own task as an extension of ritual activity in the home. "But the families of our children are not used to praying together," comes the rejoinder. Nor will they ever be . . . as long as the existing scheme continues to perpetuate itself. Children *will* respond to lively, and pleasurable, ritual experiences created for them outside of their family setting; yet if this is their *only* setting, they will breathe a certain artificiality: "prayer is part of life," we are saying to them, in a thousand different ways; and they are learning, in a more powerful way still, that common prayer belongs in school and in church, and only there.

Is it asking too much of liturgy planners whose particular focus is children to be ever-conscious of the role that is theirs in terms of helping families to pray together? The answer to this question depends on the way that these persons view the overall task they have assumed. If they see their activity with children as an end in itself, working tirelessly to create celebrations capable of involving them, then the answer is yes: work with families will take second place, and will assume the nature of an impossible burden; even the planning of family masses and other sacramental celebrations will be viewed, unconsciously perhaps, as a way to involve parents in events that are intrinsically children's events. If, however, the activity is viewed in another way, namely, as something which flows from ritual prayer and practice in the home, and leads to the public prayer of families gathered together (which, in turn, leads to the common prayer of the whole faith community), then the answer to the question is no. Viewed in this way, the task becomes less burdensome, in fact; parents are quick to sense that the total thrust of the program is in their direction, and are much more apt to become involved in the liturgy-planning process. Granted, the initial stages of the process will reflect a great deal of work on the part of the designated "planners" (CCD personnel, teachers, etc.). But gradually this will be shared by more and more parents: the effort will become one of genuine co-responsibility.

FAMILIES AT COMMON PRAYER

The persons who assume responsibility for planning family celebrations on the parochial level should plan not in terms of a month or a season, but for an entire year. Masses will be part of the overall plan, yes, as will a wide variety of non-eucharistic celebrations for various occasions, holidays, feasts (the first day of spring, perhaps, or the 4th of July, or Thanksgiving). Once again, special care should be taken in the choice of days for family masses . . . the feasts of Easter and Pentecost, for example, the First Sundays of Advent and Lent are *not* appropriate days for such celebrations. Better to choose other

Sundays in the Easter and Pentecost seasons, other Sundays of Advent and Lent . . . Christmas eve, perhaps.

The Directory for Masses with Children does, in fact, offer very helpful guidelines for celebrations of this kind. Its suggestions, as well as its cautions, are worthy of study. (The document appears as an appendix to this book.)

The assumption is often made, and wrongly so, that family celebrations have potential for the involvement only of children and their parents. While these occasions do not always lend themselves to the participation of teen-agers, they are very often satisfying experiences for childless couples, for the aged, the single, for those whose children have grown. Through failure, on the part of those planning family liturgies, to seek out these persons and to make them feel wanted and welcome it is very easy to create an air of exclusivity about an event the nature of which cries out for inclusion. This practice is a deprivation to families as well, especially those many families who are geographically distant from grandparents, aunts, uncles, cousins—all those who, in former times, lent support both to parents and to children. Children need to establish significant relationships with adults other than their parents. And parents need to know that their children are not solely dependent on them for their whole affective development. Where better for these needs to be met than in and through the parish community?

Signs, Songs and Stories attempts to serve its readers with the theoretical knowledge they will need if they wish to plan wisely and well for children, their families and their friends. It also proffers ideas, starting-points for the fuller development of themes. Throughout the essays that comprise the volume, a unity of thought and direction can be perceived: this is a rich faith tradition that we share—its authors say, over and over again—one that is grasped gradually, deeply, if presented and celebrated with beauty and with grace. A great disservice is rendered, to adults and children alike, when the banal and the contrived are considered fitting expression for the mysteries of our Christian faith.

WHERE HAVE WE BEEN, WHERE ARE WE GOING?

Is it possible to characterize developments in the realm of children's liturgies over these last five or six years with some measure of accuracy? To the best of our knowledge, surveys do not exist which provide data of this kind; unfortunately, the process of evaluation, even on a parochial level, has not known wide usage. As with the broader area of parish liturgical renewal, we are not awfully good at sharing our successes, our failures, our processes with other parishes, either on a local, diocesan or national level. The few remarks which follow reflect the personal experience of the writer of these lines, the experience of others who have contributed to *Signs, Songs and Stories* and to other Liturgical Conference publications.

In trying to determine the form which activity in children's liturgies has taken in parishes throughout the country, it appears that the focus of greatest interest is the mass, and more specifically, the liturgy of the word. The practice of "setting the children apart" from the congregation during this time, and bringing them in at the time of the presentation of gifts, is fairly widespread. It might be suggested that such a procedure is not without merit; its regular usage leaves something to be desired, as we have indicated earlier. It is based on the assumption that the liturgy of the word, as experienced by the larger assembly, precludes involvement by children . . . on any experience level. (One is reminded of the argument for the use of missalettes which include scripture readings: "If the people didn't have them, they wouldn't know what was being read.") Without belaboring the point any further, let it simply be said that if harder efforts were exerted on enlivening and enriching the liturgy of the word in our Sunday parish masses, the need for "adapting" it for children on every occasion would diminish very quickly.

Celebrations of reconciliation have also become a major focus of interest—for adults, for children, for groups of adults and children together. While celebrations of this kind, in home, classroom or church, surely have a place in children's lives, their over-use can only be deplored. May these next few years witness an awareness, on the part of all who are engaged in liturgy planning for children, of the wide and marvelous opportunities that are theirs for creating simple rituals around God's simple gifts! There is a strong tendency, even in celebrations not based on a theme of reconciliation, to moralize in a way the Bible does not . . . to transform the rich images of Old and New Testament, even of the better children's stories, into guidelines of "good" (that is, socially approved) behavior.

The past few years have witnessed the appearance of numerous books and programs designed to help the children's liturgy planner. By and large these take the form of actual scenarios, based on various themes: flowers, water, family, hope, etc. Readings are provided, songs, prayers, suggestions for gestures, and the rest. It can be guessed that the less secure, the novices, rely heavily on these helps—not merely for the words they provide, but for the actual format they suggest. It must also be said that many planning groups are well beyond this stage: they do make use of available resources for ideas, springboards for their own powers of creativity, but only that.

While many persons engaged in the work of planning children's liturgies find that they *are* creative in terms of visual and other artistic effects, in terms of seeking out songs and devising gestures which develop a particular theme, they are frustrated in their attempts to create good, and varied, liturgies. What is lacking, often, is a security about the Christian message itself: What *is* it we are celebrating? What is this biblical heritage that is ours . . . worthy of festivalizing with our children, with one another? Wherein lies the unique spirit of Jesus Christ, the meaning of discipleship?

It is to these questions, over any other, that *Signs, Songs and Stories* addresses itself. The day is drawing closer when Christians of all ages will grasp what it is that makes us delight in the Lord, that makes us one. And the discovery will signal the end of books, and all the other crutches that help us on the road to "creating" celebrations. Then we will know. It is the fond hope of all who have worked on this volume that their efforts have brought that day just a little bit closer.

—Virginia Sloyan

How Children Grow

All adults who work with children must know how to provide their youngsters with opportunities to move forward toward maturity. Leaders of children's liturgy groups are no exception. If liturgy is a celebration of life—life transformed, made new in the Lord Jesus—it certainly must aid and enhance life's natural changes.

What brings about the changes in children's feelings, actions, and growth that we call development? Nobody really knows. As a result of several decades of scientific study of children, we now have access to some facts and many theories. Quite a few mysteries remain.

This summary of children's needs and development is based on the assumption that personal growth is a complicated interweaving of biology and experience. Biology provides each child with some inner drives, with genetic codes for growth, with the sense avenues for acquiring information about the world around him.

Experience provides the stimuli which "turn on" the biological child. Experience includes affection, intellectual stimulation, nutrition, praise and criticism, color and texture, security and threats, bicycles and televisions, and all the other happenings in a person's life. Without experience, there is no activation of the child's mind and body.

At each period in a child's life there are certain problems or tasks that must be mastered if the growth toward maturity is going to continue. These "developmental tasks" result from the interaction of biological changes and the demands of experience and culture. For infants, there are developmental tasks such as learning to walk, talk, control elimination, etc. In this section we will be describing the tasks for six- to twelve-year-old children.

PHYSICAL CHANGES

Physically, six-year-old children have come a long way. They've learned to control their movements so that such complicated phenomena as walking, running, talking, drawing, throwing, etc. are now old habits. They've managed to control their bodily functions and have learned to recognize and react to the signs of fatigue, hunger, thirst, and pain.

10

After six years of rapid growth, the child's body takes on a more even course in height and weight gain. There are some spurts of change here and there over the years, just a reminder that the dramatic onset of puberty is on the way.

"Without experience, there is no activation of the child's mind and body."

After six or so years devoted to basic muscle mastery, a child's energies are now devoted to refinement. If Janie knows how to draw, she wants to learn more and more complex pictures. If Jeff knows how to run, he wants to learn the complicated running needed for soccer. You've seen the six-year-old's struggle with printing the alphabet. You've seen the hours spent on jump-rope games. You've seen the devotion to the basketball and net. All of these events are witness to the beautiful determination of each child to make his body serve as a tool for his thinking, his curiosity, his social needs.

The developmental tasks of physical growth include:
   improving the skill and control of large muscles;
   learning the skills required for organized games and sports;
   gaining control of fine muscle movements;
   developing physical prowess and athletic skills.
YOUR WORK WITH CHILDREN IN LITURGIES MUST ALLOW THEM TO WORK ON THEIR DEVELOPMENTAL TASKS IN SOME WAY.

INTELLECTUAL GROWTH

In the earliest years of thinking, a child learns that objects have permanence—that teddy bear doesn't cease to exist when baby can no longer see it. Later, small children learn that objects serve as signs for other things or events or ideas . . . toddlers know that when mother picks up the car keys, it means a trip to the store or the park. It's characteristic of young children to judge all events by their appearances; a three-year-old may say that the steam shovel eats the dirt. Also, young children are almost completely egocentric. All of these characteristics of thinking are totally natural for children under six or so years.

At about age six or seven a child's thinking makes a big leap toward maturity. The "age of reason" it is called. The Swiss psychologist Jean Piaget has thoroughly described children's thinking, calls the years from seven to eleven "the stage of concrete operations." Now the child's thinking becomes increasingly more logical and systematic. When a child encounters a situation which (s)he can't deal with because of lack of experience, (s)he is able to use analogy as a tool. (S)he is able to understand that objects are not essentially changed just because they change in size or shape or color or some other appearance.

These children now begin to realize that words do not have the power of action, that words are not the same as things, that "saying doesn't make it so." (How often you hear the phrase, "Sticks and stones can break my bones but words can never hurt me!")

Children in these elementary years can make and work with mental images, they can plan, they can predict what will happen if . . . They can organize what they know about the world and understand complex series of events, symbol systems, causes and effects, etc. Now they can think through a problem without having to "rehearse it" or act it out. They are more consistent, more logical, and much more like adults in their thinking processes.

The developmental tasks of intellectual growth include:
> learning the symbol systems (numbers, letters, reading, computing) as required by our culture;
> learning, understanding, recognizing the physical phenomena of the world;
> developing skills of memory, analogy, logic, problem-solving, creative thinking, abstraction.

YOUR WORK WITH CHILDREN IN LITURGIES MUST ALLOW THEM TO WORK ON THEIR DEVELOPMENTAL TASKS IN SOME WAY.

SOCIAL AND EMOTIONAL GROWTH

In the beginning, a baby's entire emotional world is circumscribed by the persons who provide nourishment. If baby's needs for food, warmth, physical contact, stimulation, and comfort are met in a sure, predictable manner, trust is learned. On this foundation of trust (or lack of it) will be developed all other patterns for emotional growth and personal relationships. Gradually a child learns to relate to persons other than his "nourishers" —relatives, friends, babysitters, teachers. Self-esteem grows and falters continually, and is especially critical at about age five, when the "oedipal crisis" occurs. At this point in their emotional growth, boys and girls, each in their own way, must resolve their feelings of love and possessiveness for their opposite-sex parent. As a result of resolving the problem successfully, boys learn to identify with their fathers, girls with their mothers. If the crisis isn't completely resolved, children can be left with strong feelings of inferiority.

Children of six or so years must have many opportunities to combat this sense of inadequacy by learning more and more about what they *can* do. In the same way a baby needs sucking, school-age children need to work, to be challenged to do things. Another way for a child to develop his sense of adequacy (or sense of industry, as Erik Erikson calls it) is by identifying with adults who are adequate—adults who *know* many things, and who *know how to do* many things. It is also critical for children to experience success. When a boy sees evidence of his accomplishment in a woodworking class, there can be no doubt about his adequacy. When a girl learns to ride her bike or to roller skate, she need not worry so much about her inferiority.

Socially, the years from six on are most decisive. In younger years, each child's values were determined primarily by the family. But now the peer group plays an ever more important role, and huge amounts of energy are devoted to gaining acceptance and recognition from classmates and friends. The problems of dependency, of security, of giving and taking love were once the struggles of home. Now they are worked out on the playground, in the classroom, in clubs and cliques and gangs. The code of the group becomes always more important.

Another critical emotional event during the years from six to twelve is each child's acceptance of his or her sex role in society. These years are called the "latency period," not because emotions are missing, but because the strong surges of feelings are more dormant than before—sort of a lull before the storm of puberty. But during this "quiet time" boys and girls work on accepting themselves as male or female. They investigate the roles society gives to men and women, and start to fit those roles into their own expectations for themselves.

The developmental tasks for emotional growth include:
> developing a sense of industry, leaving behind the feelings of inferiority;
> developing friendships outside the family circle and achieving a degree
> of independence from family;
> gaining acceptance and prestige from the peer group;
> finding constructive ways of dealing with frustrations, threats, anger, fear;
> learning and accepting the appropriate sex role.

YOUR WORK WITH CHILDREN IN LITURGIES MUST ALLOW THEM TO WORK ON THEIR DEVELOPMENTAL TASKS IN SOME WAY.

WAYS OF WORKING ON THE DEVELOPMENTAL TASKS

Here are some do's and don'ts, practical hints to make it easier for you to meet children's needs while planning and celebrating special liturgies which involve them.

DO allow for lots of talking, especially in the planning times. DON'T do too much talking yourself. Children need to tell you, and each other, about themselves and about their lives. They use talking to explain, and also to solve their problems. In the very process of saying what happened or how it felt, a child can come to understand and accept himself.

DO use many and varied forms of expression. DON'T get stuck in the pattern of using only word and song. Children need to explore with all of their muscles, all their senses. Are you really satisfied to use only the eyes, the ears and the vocal chords? What about tastes and smells? What about mime, acrobatics or modern dance? What about costumes, lighting effects, sound effects? What about body rhythms, body strength, the joy of moving in unison with other bodies?

"DON'T make them dependent on you . . .

DO expect children to learn from each other."

DO find each child's area of success. DON'T expect all the children to be good at everything. Point out Joyce's good singing voice, Sherman's skill at making posters, Beverly's ease with cartwheels, Jeff's ability to understand how other kids are feeling. Appreciate the variety of gifts among children, and encourage them to share your appreciation.

Do answer children's questions, no matter how silly or out of context they seem. DON'T make a child feel foolish or "bad" because of his curiosity. There is a lot that young boys and girls don't know about their feelings and their bodies; about what happens during illness; about death; about God; about the rules of society; about why and when and how and where. You must share with them what you know, and give them the opportunity to use that tool we call knowledge.

DO allow the children to love you. DON'T make them dependent on you. Children, like all of us, need to love and be loved. The form of love they need now is trust, acceptance, limits, challenges, encouragement. We don't honor their growth needs by making ourselves the focal point for affection or the source of all favors.

DO expect children to learn from each other. DON'T expect to be their only source of values and information. Remember, this is the time when peers become ever more important.

DO realize that what children want most of all is to be accepted. DON'T sentimentalize childhood as the "wonderful, enchanting, golden years." Children, like the rest of us, also know moments of loneliness, boredom, fear, and hostility. If they learn from us to understand and accept all their feelings, they will have the best chance for constant self-esteem.

DO allow (within limits) for frivolity, play, exploration in your groups. DON'T be overly serious and "product" oriented. The process by which you and the children develop celebrations can itself be a celebration of growth.

This section was written by Meg Reisett, who is Director of the Montgomery County (Maryland) Community Coordinated Child Care Council and is professionally trained in Montessori methods and human development.

The Prayer Of Children

Perceiving the Unapparent

Prayer presumes a sense of the presence of God and the accessibility of images that serve to establish and evoke the relationship between the person of man and the person of the divine. Generally speaking, our culture lacks both the sense of presence and the accessibility of such images . . .

It seems to me that the problem with prayer in all of us is that our vision of the world has been reduced to the point where reality is a one dimensional, univocal banality . . . We, as a culture, have become so unperceptive that we really think things are as they appear to be through some commonsense, unimaginative absorption of the data of our experience. Reality has become a technological bore, where the supreme virtue is to conform to the dull products of a latter-day Puritan ethic: a product of a Cartesian worldview, now lying dead and putrefying.

Where prayer is reduced to an act of duty it is effectually torn from its roots. It no longer draws its nourishment from the deep sense of God's presence in the events of our life and it becomes something one does out of a caricature of the categorical imperative. Prayer is an act of love. How successful is love-making done by command? Prayer is a spontaneous expression of adoration and confession, thanksgiving and petition, and ultimately the inexpressible "more." Is it not true that the letter of the law kills, while the spirit gives life?

The presupposition of a living prayer life, which can carry itself without being shored up by a sense of duty—namely, a sense of the presence of God and the accessibility of images to establish and evoke the relationship—begins in our earliest months of life. It is the fruit of a family in which the parents themselves live in the light of an enchanted world. Such a light reveals things to us not only in their surface appearance, but also in their relationship to us, so that we know what they are. We see not just the "landscape," but what Gerald Manley Hopkins called the "inscape."

THE SENSE OF PRESENCE

Let me speak of the sense of presence. Erik Erikson, the eminent psychoanalyst, has written of the symbol of the mother's breast to an infant-in-arms. He points out that the breast is not just a means for conveying physical nourishment, but that it becomes for the baby, however subliminally, a singular representation of the "cosmic breast," that nourishing mystery upon which all life is founded. The child's experience of a human breast as his initial contact with the world becomes an immensely significant symbol for him in his grasp of the nature of the world into which he has been involuntarily thrust. It is tempting to suggest a correlation between the breast-feeding of babies and mysticism, but even without the support of such an incredible research project the point has not gone without some related verification (e.g. in the studies of Harlow on apes and of Spitz on English children in World War II).

A sense of presence is built upon an expectancy of life—an expectation that things are more wonderful than they appear. I am fond of saying that you cannot really believe in Santa Claus until you have gone through the process of believing, not-believing, and then believing again. My father was the town Santa Claus in the thirties. Every Christmas he came down the Methodist Church steeple—quite a feat, since he was able to fulfill Clement Clarke Moore's image without additional padding—much to the delight of the town children. On one occasion a neighbor's child, needing to appear more intelligent than the rest, declared in a loud voice that the man in the red suit was not really Santa Claus but Dr. Holmes. My clear recollection of my father's post-performance reaction was that this childhood indiscretion was not only a violation of the children's fantasy world, but was in fact an *untruth*! For that time he was Santa Claus, as the priest who stands at the altar is Christ!

Those of us who live in an enchanted world, in which prayer is the inevitable response to an awareness of the extraordinary within the ordinary, must be able to think as the little child who is allowed to be a little child. I have always been very much bothered by people who want their children to have only "educational toys." What this suggests to me is that they want their children to play so that they can perform efficiently in the society in which they live. Prayer is not built upon efficient performance, but upon the ability to dream and to be an interpreter of dreams. In one sense we can say that the task is to develop an esthetic sensitivity in our children, and not a technological mind set.

"Prayer is built upon the ability to dream . . . "

Parents who want their children to pray have to pray themselves. I do not mean in private nor do I mean, *necessarily*, in any structured liturgical sense. What I am suggesting is that they have to live as persons who are in constant dialog with the unapparent mystery of life. Examples of this are the uninhibited joy we express in our physical love, the obvious delight in the fellowship of a meal, the compassionate concern we share in the presence of pain and sickness, and the genuine repugnance we declare before evil. Our emotions—joy, delight, concern, and repugnance—more than our thinking stimulate in our children the sense of God's presence in the ordinary events of life.

Recently I was visiting for a few days with a Methodist clergyman and his family in Montana. Their whole life seemed to me imbued with the beauty of the country in which they lived. He had begun his ministry in Yellowstone Park and his wife had been brought up in a family whose father was in the park service. A sense of joy in creation flooded over in a number of ways in their life, particularly at meals. They sang their grace each meal and their two young boys, aged six and four, lost themselves in the delight of the moment. There was no sense of doing a duty to thank God, but of sharing with the creator who was an obvious member of the number assembled. Despite the public pronouncement of their own denomination, the pleasure with which they *all* drank their wine at the big meal of the day reminded me of Paul Tillich's explanation of the symbolic power of wine. On one occasion, after expostulating about the vitality of wine, Tillich was asked by a Southern Baptist student whether or not grape juice was just as good. He made a "bad face" in response and exclaimed, "Grape juice! My God, have you ever tasted it!"

THE ACCESSIBILITY OF IMAGES

Now let me speak concerning the accessibility of images. Of course, a sense of presence requires images that can convey an awareness of this presence, and for the last few pages I have intentionally shared with the reader a number of such images, hoping that they would evoke in him a feeling of the presence of which I was speaking. There is a need, however, to speak directly about the whole imagery of prayer in order to encourage us not to shrink from sharing this with our children.

An image is for me something within our environment (body, memory, culture, tradition) that has the possibility of becoming a symbol and thus of clarifying the relationship between ourselves and our experience—in this instance, God. Prayer without symbols, prayer in which the words represent only the structures and opinions of our social world, is flat and powerless. Prayer must be made up of images that are charged with mystery and describe and evoke the experience that transcends our univocal, secular existence.

Such an image begins, it seems to me, with the parents of a child kneeling at the crib of their infant. It is given substance by the traditional prayers of our faith: the Lord's Prayer, the *Gloria Patri*, the *Te deum*, the *Gloria in excelsis*, and (if it be a part of your tradition) the Hail, Mary. I see no reasonable objection and many reasons for memorizing these. Furthermore, the young child needs at a very early age to be exposed to and encouraged to assimilate the Christian story, with all the images that it carries. The Christian year shared within family ritual does this so very well, as does the reading of the scriptures.

The point is that the natural imagination of the young child needs to be fed with images that have the possibility of becoming for him the spontaneous symbolic expression of a relation that he dimly perceives with God. Such symbols carry within them the hermeneutical power to deepen and sharpen the sense of God's presence and become the foundation upon which a realistic prayer life can develop. My spiritual director in seminary was fond of saying that the mind becomes the color of its thoughts, and that in our moments of relaxed reflection we will call upon those thoughts most deeply embedded within it. He loved to tell the story of the old person who, as she lay dying, could only repeat, "Now I lay me down to sleep, I pray the Lord my soul to keep." How fitting, he pointed out, that those words, probably the first she memorized so many years before, returned to her consciousness to accompany her to the presence of our Lord.

Perhaps this seems a bit sentimental to the reader. Indeed it can be, if we let it be only a frosting on the cake of an otherwise banal existence in a vapid world, and given over to the worship of a domesticated God. Prayer needs to grapple with mystery, and this means that in prayer both we and our children must come to see in life the profoundly humorous and the profoundly horrible, to know that prayer can be a controlled form of rage or of ecstasy. If we as adults think that God is shocked by our laughter or does not know our terror, if we are ashamed of our anger before injustice or our delight in our body and the bodies of others, let us not seduce our children into believing in such an eviscerated, sentimental religion. Books have been (and more should be) written on this. Here I only wish to note that Satan today probably appears to us as sheer banality, and that the most powerful symbols of our experience of God lie in the incongruity of humor and horror, as well as the uncontrolled venting of passion. Prayer is passion—love and suffering in the face of the divine.

It seems to me that we need to explore with children the nature of their passion. The child naturally loves "ghost stories," he laughs with utter abandon, he is capable of the most incredible rage, and loves without inhibition. If we did not teach him to repress all in this which makes us uncomfortable in our controlled little world, and instead encouraged him to see in his passion the power that is there without becoming lost in chaos, we would have a great mine of images for prayer. Medieval man called natural deformities "monsters" from the Latin word, *monstrate*, meaning to "demonstrate." They "demonstrated" to his mind the presence of God. In more than one culture comedy, even ribaldry, has been seen as an occasion for revelation.

Of course, the central and indispensable symbol for Christian prayer is Christ.

We pray *in the name of Christ*. That means, however, in the power of him who is the primal symbol of God for us. Jesus is no "pale Galilean," no flat, sweet, inoffensive, passive dependent, incapable of passion. Born in a stinking barn, reared as one of the people of the earth, familiar with toilsome sweat and peasant humor, he came to a gruesome crucifixion as a common criminal. There is a symbol of the presence of God to man awesomely potent in its very incongruity! It is in the growing knowledge of such a rebel that our children's prayer life should develop.

NEITHER LICENSE NOR LAW

Too many people today see child-rearing as an alternative between so-called "permissivism" and discipline. By the former I assume they mean license, or letting the child have his own way, and by the latter I gather they mean forming the child by the application of the law. I think both approaches miss the point completely. Perhaps what I have written here will be interpreted by some as an approach to children and prayer out of a spirit of "permissivism." It is not what I intend.

Children assimilate and accommodate themselves to what they see happening around them. What the child "sees" is, as a matter of fact, conditioned by what others lead the child to see. Children take what is gathered, and if it has the possibility of making sense, it becomes the meaning in terms of which they live their lives. This is an organic process, by which we become what we incorporate, which is joined to an innate need to be "somebody," to be a person we ourselves value. I would identify this with the development of the ego, or the self taking responsibility for self. Prayer is a part of this dialog with the world, in terms of which a Christian seeks to become one with Christ and to become fully human as Christ is human.

My point is that this is a process that comes on *within* an individual, in the context of an environment that both stimulates such development and provides the necessary material for its growth. The goal is to achieve a personhood that is supported by its own internal skeletal structure, and not one supported, like an insect, by an external shell. The emphasis is on the *internal* process in dialog with the world, a world in which God encounters us, calls us, and gives us his strength. This is not possible without prayer. The end result is, hopefully, a grace-filled, self-authenticating person "in Christ."

Roy Lee, an English priest and student of Freud, speaks of this internalized religion as "ego religion." It is obviously not the result of "permissivism," nor is it the end product of an obsession with discipline. The latter, he effectively argues, produces a rigid, unproductive, and lifeless "superego religion." Inasmuch as it is an imposed structure, unresponsive to a person's need to make subtle, ethical distinctions and often to transcend the wisdom of our structure, it becomes a guilt-provoking straitjacket. Where the life of faith is the result of such imposed standards, always arbitrarily and, inevitably, inadequately conceived, the end result is a dutiful worship of a God who is little more than a remote policeman and jailor combined. Such a God is appropriate to a Puritan ethic, for he is more sovereign judge than lover. The incarnation becomes a very weak possibility for us, and one is left wondering what point of contact in this world he may find between God and man in prayer. Indeed, prayer often becomes so many lifeless words, uttered out of a sense of duty begotten of fear to a God off somewhere, out of reach.

It strikes me, if an Anglican may speak to some of his readers that are of the Roman Catholic tradition, that the fervor with which so many people have said the Hail, Mary is begotten of a childhood fantasy in which the stern Father was unapproachable and the best recourse one had was to Mother. A healthy prayer life might not abandon the Hail, Mary, but an "ego religion" might more appropriately center itself in the reality of God-become-man in Jesus of Nazareth, the God who came not to condemn people, but out of love to save them.

More important, a "superego religion" is by its very nature captured in the society in which we live. The prayer of such religion is permeated by a sense of obligation to support the *status quo*. If prayer is to be what Matthew Fox has rightly suggested it ought to be, a response to life in which we confront life's enemies as well as enjoying life, then our children cannot see it as an act of submission to a God who is a cosmic projection of the perceived, rigid order of society. Prayer has to be the context in which we can play with the possibilities of a new life, in which the old injustice can be done away with in God's name.

Prayer must have for our children and ourselves social consequences, which are made possible because it locates us in a relationship with God in which we are not coerced to endure the present, but invited into a new future. This is why I suggest that prayer taught as an obligation to our children raises serious problems, and that it is better understood as the same kind of ludic event, filled with wonderful images and excitement, as is exemplified in "playing house" or "doctor." Here the child can listen to God, develop a perception of reality that is relatively free of the identification of the society with God, and find a transcendental motivation for identifying and fighting the diabolical that lurks within every institution, no matter how sacrosanct.

I am aware that there is a certain idealism, as well as imprecision, in this discussion. This is to a measure intentional. Prayer itself is an act of trust, a conversation which characterizes a pilgrimage or exploration. It involves the kind of risk necessary, if we are to grow beyond what others would have us be, and become that for which God has created us. This is why I speak of it more as the result of a developed sense of the presence of God and the ability to build a self-understanding before him in terms of the accessible images. My emphasis is upon the maturation of a person who is free, responsible, and accountable; and yet, because he is so open to God's presence within him, he is ultimately a mystery to himself.

It strikes me that children are particularly susceptible to that understanding of prayer, if we but guide them and yet not stifle their God-given proclivities. Perhaps it was that to which our Lord was referring when he suggested that to enter the kingdom of heaven is to become as a little child.

This section was written by Urban T. Holmes, Dean of the School of Theology at the University of the South, Sewanee, Tennessee; he is the author of many articles and books, including Young Children and the Eucharist *(Seabury).*

Learning "By Heart"

When a preliminary draft of the bishops' *Basic Teachings* document was sent to various consultors, many of us looked with dismay at the list of prayer-forms considered part of a Catholic's essential equipment. It included not only the Our Father, Hail Mary, and Apostles' Creed (fair enough), but also the "Acts" of Faith, Hope, Charity, and Contrition. We remembered our own struggle as children to memorize these abstract and wordy formulas and our more recent unhappy efforts as parents or teachers to help children memorize them. Happily, they were dropped from the final version. But in discussing the draft document, I found that a number of parents and catechists were opposed to children's learning *any* prayer-forms, on the grounds that doing so blocked their spontaneity, led to meaningless repetition, and so on. It seems to me that this is a dangerously one-sided position.

I would certainly agree that children should not be forced to memorize prayers, or to recite them so that we can be sure they can do so correctly. But there is no need to sit down and painfully "commit them to memory." Children do not need to memorize the names of their immediate families; they have become "familiar" with them. We don't force children to learn the words of "Happy birthday to you"; they come to know them from singing them at birthdays. Most children, in fact, have much better verbal memories than we give them credit for: witness their ability to recite the latest TV ads, especially if these are sung and in some kind of verse-form.

WE NEED A STOREHOUSE

So I think that they should be given ample opportunities to become familiar with worthy prayer-forms (including, of course, hymns) in such a way that, without conscious effort, they do learn them "by heart." And "by heart"— in the biblical sense of the center of thinking, feeling and willing—is how prayers should be learned. It seems to me, then, that the greater the treasury of Christian prayers we can familiarize them with during their growing years, the better they will be equipped to mature in praying in later life.

For worthy prayer-forms not only give us words to pray with but also educate us in praying. When the disciples asked Jesus, "Lord, teach us to pray," his response was at once a prayer-form and a lesson in the attitude we should have in praying and what to pray for. In the same way, for example, the psalms—which, as a stoic friend who objected to them once said, "are full of moaning and groaning"—not only give us phrases in which to express our own moans and groans, but also show us that we can and should cry out to God out of the depths, any depths.

Moreover, we need a storehouse of familiar prayers and prayer-phrases that will supply our hearts and lips with appropriate expressions beyond what we ourselves are capable of, and so help us articulate to ourselves what aspect of our deepest personhood we are trying to open to God. We need them, too, just because they *are* familiar, and so provide a sense of continuity with our own past and with that of the whole church, and help satisfy our human need for ritual, that is, for doing something in an accustomed way.

BEYOND THE OBVIOUS

But to serve these purposes, the prayers with which we offer children opportunities to become deeply familiar must be "poetic-simple," as opposed to "poetic-difficult" and, still more, to "scientific-simple" and "scientific-difficult." (These categories are described in Canon Drinkwater's essay, "The Use of Words: A Problem of Both Content and Method," in *Shaping the Christian Message*, ed. by Gerard S. Sloyan, The Macmillan Co., 1958. The author says, with great charm and conviction, that only the "poetic-simple" should be used in preaching or catechesis.)

By "poetic" here is meant the combination of words and word-music and the images or symbols they express—enhanced by the melody and other musical elements in the case of hymns—which have the power to convey meaning beyond what can be conceptualized or verbalized. Such meaning can be sensed by children, adolescents and adults, each on his or her own level, and keep on inviting them to reach out from where they are to "the Beyond in the midst."

"Let all your works give you praise, O Lord . . . "

In other words, this quality essential to prayers and hymns which speak to our hearts, and which we can pray from our hearts, rules out the "simple" that is merely banal, that does not stretch our imaginations, and arouse wonder and awe. This kind of simplicity stifles rather than fosters children's innate ability to appreciate or create images that convey meanings beyond the obvious. And in so doing it cripples children's ability to be aware of and responsive to the Presence which is in and beyond the here and now; it inhibits prayer.

Unfortunately, many good people do not know the difference between the poetic-simple and the banal. Moreover, we have all become aware of the futility, if not the harmfulness, of forcing abstract statements on children which they cannot understand and so mis-understand. But we tend to apply this to areas in which conceptual understanding is not essential. A young child can only make fantasized nonsense, if anything, out of an abstract phrase like "Supreme Being infinite in all perfections." But it does not follow that (s)he cannot experience wonder, delight, and infinite caringness when hearing or praying Psalm 23, or its paraphrase, the hymn, "The King of Love my shepherd is."

"and let your faithful ones bless you."

Psalm 145

PRAYER AND IMAGINATION

One objection, frequently raised today about many traditional Christian prayers and, in particular, the psalms, is that modern urban children have no experience of the kind of rural culture(s) out of which they emerged and, consequently, the images—such as those of sheep and shepherd—are meaningless to them. In my own experience, this objection is not a valid one. The first school I attended was Protestant-oriented, with a morning assembly at·which we prayed short psalms in the King James version, including "The Lord is my shepherd" and "I will lift mine eyes unto the hills," and sang hymns such as "America the Beautiful." It didn't bother me at all that I had never had any firsthand contact with any sheep or seen any hills higher than those around Boston and the southern coast of Maine—let alone "purple mountains' majesty above the fruited plain." I felt delighted and awed and drawn out of myself; I think I really prayed.

But—and this is a very important "but"—I had been read a variety of legends and stories involving sheep and mountains and many other real and fantastic creatures, and gazed at their illustrations; my imagination had been fostered and fed. It seems to me that such fostering through poetic-simple stories is a necessity in children's upbringing very closely connected with helping them learn to pray. And modern children have the added advantage of a great deal of secondhand experience, through watching TV and Westerns in particular, of the kind of country and situations described in many of the psalms (e.g., "O God, my Rock and my Refuge").

Poetic-simple prayers are to be found in many different places—the writings of holy men and women, the liturgies of East and West, many books of the Bible. I would not attempt a list here even of psalms or selections from psalms, which might be appropriate to one or another age level or situation except to say: Don't be as afraid of giving children too rich a diet as of undernourishing them in this regard.

MAKE THEM YOUR OWN

But one more aspect of introducing children to worthy prayers seems to me worth mentioning; it must be done, as far as you can manage it, in a prayerful and poetic-simple fashion. Make sure first that you have made them *your own prayers* and can pray them as such, and that you can pray them aloud prayerfully and in such a way as to bring out their basic cadences and word-music. I would recommend, I think, that the children first follow your praying a given prayer or singing a hymn, and pray it with you, or join in praying it with an adult group. Then give any explanations you think might be helpful—for example, in connection with Psalm 23, some pictures and information about the Palestinian style of sheep-herding and oriental customs of hospitality—and then ask the children to pray it again. Further possibilities, for older children, would be to ask them to think of experiences of their own in which someone's caring and protecting produced trustfulness, and to tell about or draw or dance or enact such experiences, and, perhaps, make up a psalm of their own based on such experiences.

Finally, I am strongly convinced that thus familiarizing children with prayers that can serve them through life, rather than with ones they will have to discard with childish things, will encourage spontaneity in prayer, and nourish it, through familiarizing them with the marvelous variety of ways in which the Lord invites us to speak with him, and of appropriate and beautiful forms in which to do it. Praying prayer-forms and praying spontaneously are not opposed, but complementary. The better we can help children and ourselves to do the one, the easier it will be to help them do the other.

This section was written by Mary Perkins Ryan, author of numerous books and articles. Ms. Ryan presently serves as executive editor of Focus on Adults *and associate editor of* Pace.

Telling The Bible Story

"What Kind of a Story Is This?"

The best homily I ever experienced is still being preached by a brick! This brick, found in Jerusalem a century ago, fascinates the children who visit the Harvard Semitic Museum even more than the macabre glitter of our gold-covered mummy of a 5000-year-old rat. At the same time, it confirms the prejudices of our archeologists who justify their exhausting research with the conviction that objects tell stories. For this brick tells a small but very real part of the greatest story:

Into its wet clay, the brickmakers had proudly stamped their mark: *LEXFR*, the abbreviation for *Legio Decima Fretensis*. The tenth "thunderbolt" legion, Caesar's favorite troops, had conquered Britain some 60 years before coming to occupy Palestine at the time that Jesus was playing children's games in Nazareth. From its Jerusalem garrison a few years later, the tenth legion would have provided the execution squad to carry out orders of the day issued by Pontius Pilate.

Archeologically such Roman military issue stampings are no rarities, but for youngsters (to many of whom the crucifix's familiarity has rendered it almost invisible) this brick suddenly shows that the central act of God's love is an event of our history. To touch reflectively the handiwork of those who knew not what they were doing makes us wonder if we do.

The best homily I ever *heard*—the only one I remember verbatim—was sighed out by an enormously fat priest, mopping his brow as fans whirred in the basement of a church in the slums: "Today's so hot I won't say anything more about the gospel than this: for goodness' sake get some ice-cream on your way home and share it with the people next door."

What God does in our history, thereby revealing to us the nature of the human situation—and our appropriate response to this good news (as illustrated here by the brick and the ice-cream)—epitomize the twofold teaching purpose and content of the scriptures, of the liturgy, and of all genuine religious instruction.

"So it came to pass . . . " and *" . . . Go and do likewise"* are vitally and inextricably linked to make up the good news we are commanded to spread. Since so little of the news we can tell children about the world at the end of the twentieth century is good, telling them of God within the context of

what his son has done for us—and proposed that we do in memory of him—
is a blessing for us all.

Because of the richly mysterious character of both the Bible and children, we
shall limit ourselves here to brief practical consideration of three large areas:

(a) the interrelationship between biblical texts and our celebration of them
within the liturgy;

(b) the point of view of children and how we might be able to deal
honestly with their honest questions;

(c) some of the ways in which the good news is told in the Bible itself
which might be appropriately adapted today.

GOD'S WORD, OUR RESPONSE

In the liturgies we celebrate with children all our fantasy and skill should be
brought into play to waken hearts to sing and hands to clap in his presence.
Yet our efforts must be guided by a deep understanding of the Bible's meaning. The tragedies of sectarianism—the old story of how the well-intentioned
exclusively accent some truths to the neglect of others and thereby divide
his people—should have their impact on the hearts of sincere disciples who
call themselves "messengers." This gospel title for us is important, for while
we are commanded to teach, we are not given the title of "teacher." We
have only one teacher, Jesus, whose violent threat about a stumbling block
(*skandalon*) warns us against tripping up the young by cluttering their
approach to him.

If out of a genuine realization of the power of God's word we can share with
children a loving respect for the scriptures and a zestful familiarity with them,
then we have taught them how to be nourished and have given them nourishment as well.

One way to do this is to include in our liturgies, from time to time, one
of the great variety of ceremonies which through the centuries believers
have used to express their reverence for the revealed word of God. With
fantasy, taste, and practical adaptation to the age, the circumstances, and
talents of the children and families we serve, these rituals can teach much
more effectively than words about the special nature of his work spoken
to us.

Within the liturgical celebration we can venerate the scriptures by: processions
to the enthroned book; processions with the book to pulpits or special places
of proclamation; acts of veneration—bowing before the book; kissing the book;
signing with the cross first the book and then oneself; standing as the gospel
is about to be read; incensing the book and its reader; elevating the book in
blessing.

Prior to the liturgical celebration we can: lavishly decorate the book, its
cover and stand (children's banners continue the ancient tradition of illuminat-

ing texts); decorate the church, especially the sanctuary and doorways, with picture stories from the text (often astoundingly appropriate, as when Gabriel would be portrayed on one side of the sanctuary arch and Mary on the other so that the liturgical activity performed beneath their images would be seen as a continuation both of the heavenly message: "The Lord is with you," and her response, "Be it done . . . "); on special occasions, use special decoration in accordance with the seasonal texts (thus in German countries, pine branches and pussy willows on Palm Sunday to recreate the spontaneously improvised royal welcome, or *Fastentüche*, sheets hung over the statues in Lent, brightly painted like comic strips with the story of salvation according to the Lenten readings).

Specially rendered proclamations of scripture can be effective: solemn incantations, the use of ancient languages or archaic vernaculars may be inappropriate today, except on special occasions when strange tongues might serve to illustrate the antiquity and universality of our message to youngsters more appreciative of sound than adults; careful, reverent reading aloud of scripture is of paramount importance (how well children can read with preparation can be heard on recordings made by the Kings College Chapel Choir or the Vienna Choir Boys); long readings (sermon on the mount or the account of the last supper) might prove helpful to children provided the translation employed is straightforward, as in *Good News for Modern Man*. (In Bavaria each Christmas Eve, even the youngest are spellbound when, before the sharing of the gifts, the head of the family opens the Bible by candlelight to read the tale which starts: "In those days a decree went forth from Caesar Augustus . . . ")

The prayers before and after the reading: perhaps overfamiliarity and haste have deadened the awesome greeting: "The Lord be with you"; children's liturgies—in fact, all liturgies—should lovingly accent those brief blessings and acclamations which surround his word and say so much so simply.

Because of the ambiguity and complexity of the many strands out of which the scriptures are woven, we are compelled, particularly with small children, to paraphrase and sometimes to explain. But we should realize that in our own retelling of God's mighty acts, in our faithful summaries of his message, in our own embellishing and updating of the metaphors of the Bible, and our dramatizing in plays and songs the tales of its heroes and weaklings, we are praying. In our illustrating, translating, re-presenting of God's word we are very much at prayer.

Ignatius of Loyola taught the exercise of imaginatively "fleshing out" the details of biblical scenes. He even proposed the olfactory dimension—attempting to reproduce in imagination the various aromas and stenches of the Orient! "The Lord of the Dance," *Godspell's* finger dance of the good Samaritan, Peter Canisius' wordless picture-catechism—indeed countless masterpieces of the visual and musical arts—serve as examples to stimulate our imaginative sharing within liturgies celebrated with children.

THE GREAT QUESTIONS

According to Andrew Lang, the author of the rainbow-hued fairy tale books, children ask of any story the question: "Is it true?" Some years ago Professor J. R. R. Tolkien, from the experiences he had enjoyed when telling his own Hobbit tales aloud to children, suggested that while this question is asked and should not be glibly passed over, children usually demand answers to two more immediate questions: The first of these often phrased in the words "Is it true?" really means "What kind of a story is this? With what am I being faced here?" The second is: "What am I supposed to think about what the people in the story *did*?"

Rather than living in a world bereft of fantasy, children today—reared in the realms of post-Disney cartoons, outer-space sagas, Sesame Street monsters, petroleum tigers, and detergent genies—have had to confront more literary genres than ever have been employed before in the history of communication. Children have developed flexible "filtering systems" so that they can analyze and parody the most sophisticated sales pitch, and in the next moment suspend all rational belief to be swept up into an exciting story of a human penguin's assault on a bat cave.

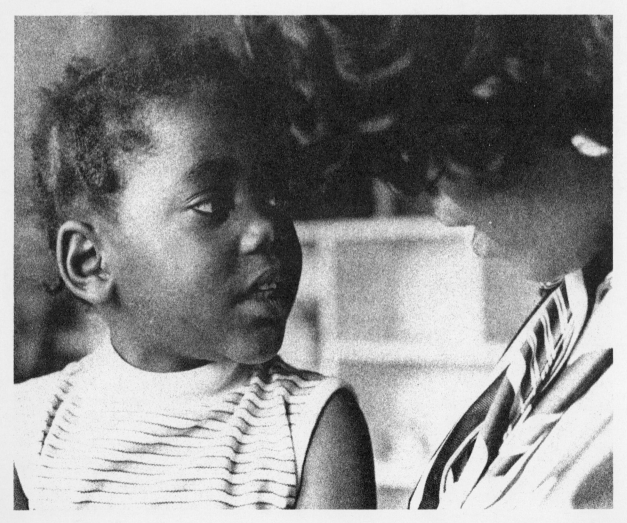

The facile ability of children to enjoy yet not really believe, coupled with their shrewd awareness of the ulterior purposes behind most of the images presented to them today, have produced a difficulty that must be recognized in our efforts of evangelization: a surfeit of stories. Even the daily news and TV specials (especially official broadcasts adorned with the flags, statues, drapes, and the solemn tones of American secular religion) confirm in children the realization that their minds and hearts are constantly being manipulated, and that the crassest exploitation is often the most cleverly disguised. As they come on to adolescence they begin to think of life as one big "commercial," a series of efforts by the adult world to sell them on something.

Yet the need for the seed of the gospel to be sown, with its real values rather than false values, has never been greater. The terror of childhood doubts has increased with family instability, the impersonalism of society, and those lurking ecological and nuclear cataclysms that the better among their teachers are alerting them to.

In view of the justified suspiciousness of children whose critical discrimination has been heightened by today's false visions, we should openly discuss with them our frank but informed opinions about the meaning of individual biblical passages. In the liturgies we celebrate with them we will be sharing the religious meaning of the Bible. This provides no assurance that the keener among them will not be having difficulties in another order. It is the most natural thing in the world, given their Western mentality and the spirit of critical inquiry that surrounds them.

The best physicians are those unafraid to say: "We don't really know for sure, but it would seem that . . . " Such an attitude in biblical matters will reveal our truthfulness and our respect for both God's word and the word of our children. The good news is ultimately beyond our total comprehension. In the area of what can be comprehended much should be shared, provided the interest is there and the questions do not hinder the search for the religious meaning of the scriptures.

Even seemingly straightforward biblical passages present real problems to a perceptive adolescent who is curious as to what the readings mean: When and where did Jesus or Paul or the prophets exaggerate for effect? When if ever did they mean harsh and contradictory words to have their literal force? While biblical commentaries can help us in this, some of these questions plunge us into areas obscure even for specialists: intertestamental apocalyptic, Jerusalem cult polemic, royal propaganda, early church redactions. Since years of linguistic and historical research usually produce still more questions but few answers in these areas, it is necessary that as we try to explain and answer the questions of the young, we realize that the service of the word is a celebration and not a graduate seminar.

There are few better human words than those of the creed to tell simply but fully the story of who, where, and why we are; whence and whither we go; what God has done, is doing, and will do for us. The creed is our perennial answer to: "Is it true? What is true? How is it true?"

"IS HE GOOD?"

The other question which Professor Tolkien found that children asked him—more frequently than "Is it true," even in its sense of "What kind of story is this?"—reflects the ability of children to enter into the action of a well-told tale: "Is he good?" "Was she being bad?" Children need to know which side to take.

Contrived moralizing tales can utterly bore children caught up in real-life struggle with evil. Our stories which "have a moral" are marked by a shallowness which children soon penetrate, whether the ulterior purpose of an individual tale be the production of dedicated young workers for Soviet industry, Chinese collectives, or sectarian religion. Faithfully telling the Bible's stories and honestly grappling with the real moral questions raised by them—this is our task, if we are trying to convey truths about human nature and the divine mercy.

In the Bible, David and Peter are at times very good and at other times very weak—just like ourselves—just as each child knows himself, or herself, to be.

In ways not unlike the vitally real virtues taught by the adventures of Huckleberry Finn, the "morals" of Bible stories are invariably subversive of the legalistic establishmentarianism which produces cautionary tales. Apparent goodness and recognition by society are constantly exposed by the Bible as "covers" for inner wickedness. Innocence is shown as maligned and exploited. The genuine virtue of the moral outcast is the Bible's *leitmotiv*.

Both testaments of scripture are not only severe in criticizing and exposing those who consider themselves to be religious and justified by the blind adherence to external conventions. Time and again the ultimate fact that God alone can judge is revealed by paradoxes and "unfair" pronouncements which prove that his thoughts are not ours. All of us must sympathize with bustling Martha as her sister simply sits, or with the good brother who was not prodigal, or with those harvesters whose sweating all day earned only as much as those hired for the last hour.

"God is good—we are weak but blessed" is always one true answer to children's questions about the moral character of figures in the Bible. The dynamic forces of God's goodness at work through human weakness is the "moral" of the Bible and our lives.

WAYS THE BIBLE TELLS ITS STORY

The message of scripture, "So it came to pass . . . " and " . . . Go and do likewise," has been communicated in many ways which say little to us now.

Today's arguments based on statistics and computerized poll results could in no way persuade an ancient people who saw themselves as specially set apart or a tiny remnant amid a foolish world. So too ancient numerology based on the significance of totals such as 40 or seven and the symbolism of sums contained within words or names, where each Hebrew or Greek letter had a numerical value, can make no sense to us. (That was true, at least, until the recent resurgence of interest in magic and the occult.) Only scholars can learn from the Bible's exhaustive listing of tribes and genealogies, structural dimensions and building materials, way stations, garrison cities, and frontier posts, or meticulously specific rules about every aspect of daily life.

Still, the genius of scriptural storytelling can teach us almost as much as those stories themselves. Let us look briefly at five ways in which God's message was communicated by the authors and editors of the Bible—in order to incorporate these skills into our own storytelling within children's liturgies.

1. *Slogans.* The joyous command "Alleluia" (Praise God!), the Bible's closing words: "Come Lord Jesus!," or "The Word was made flesh and dwelt among us," and dozens of other short phrases epitomize the good news and crystallize our purpose, our hope, and our faith.

Biblical names tell stories, often the whole story, in one word intensely personal to children who bear these names or know them: Michael (Who is like God?), Gabriel (My mighty warrior is God), Raphael (God heals), Joseph (It is God who makes things grow).

Children, fascinated by the mystery of names, carefully choose names for pets and toys and can easily appreciate the Bible's emphasis on name-giving. This is true whether parents are shown immortalizing special circumstances surrounding a birth or God is shown shaping destiny by giving a new name. To be sure, some biblical names mean little: Deborah (bee), Mary (chubby?), Thomas (twin). However, even when scholars are quite sure in some cases that ancient derivations are not entirely accurate, the Bible's editors constantly sought to fix tales and characters into our memory by explaining the meaning of names— even by atrocious puns. Such name-explanations were applied to places, often poignantly as in the case of Jerusalem (City of Peace) or Golgotha (Skull Place).

Islamic tradition teaches that God has 100 names (the Mighty, the Judge, the Compassionate, etc.), but we know only 99, for the hundredth name is known only to God Himself. Thus the Muslim world expresses the impossibility of reducing the nature of God to human formulas. Similar reverence before God's name (often read simply as "the Name") characterizes the Bible, yet each of God's biblical names or titles communicates a pregnant truth: *YHWH* (He who brings into being that which is), *El Elyon* (God is the most high), *El Sabbaoth* (The Lord is the God of the celestial armies).

Jesus' titles, *Immanuel* (God is with us), the Christ (the Anointed, Messiah), Son of God and Son of Man, encapsulate the whole story—as does most especially his name Jesus=Joshua=Jehoshua (It is God who saves us).

For the meanings of names a book such as John L. McKenzie's *Dictionary of the Bible* (Macmillan, 1965) can prove enormously helpful to shapers of children's liturgies. But not only for names. At the root of our abstract theological terms lie very concrete Hebrew words. Salvation, redemption, love, faith, truth, and many more concepts should be checked in such a book in preparation for a liturgy celebrating such a theme. To know that Jesus means "God saves us" can help a child. Yet much clearer and more accurate is the realization that the greatest of names seems to signify literally "It is God who pulls us out of the hole"!

Such names are more than theological statements. They are prayers—acts of faith, hope and often thanksgiving—whose power and preciousness can be discovered by children and encourage them to create their own short prayerful statements. Some of these will be seen as old as the good news itself and as fresh as the moment of giving a new name.

2. *Capsule Summaries*. Besides many Old Testament poetic metaphors expressing the eternal love story (the songs of the vineyard, the suffering servant, the divine bridegroom) and the pithy résumés of the good news attributed to Peter and Paul in the book of Acts and found in the letters to the young churches, Jesus himself frequently outlines the whole story for us in a few words, as in the beatitudes, the Lord's prayer, and his great command of love.

A particularly moving summary of the good news is the ancient Israelite's creed: "When your son asks you who you are, tell him: 'My father was a wandering Aramean whom God called forth' . . . " While this story summarizes our common heritage, each child could be encouraged to compose a parallel story telling of God's goodness in ages past and now—a personal answer to that most basic question "Who are you?"

3. *Images*. Cabbages and kings, those agricultural and political presuppositions which underlie most biblical metaphors, are in fact comprehensible even to young urban citizens of a twentieth-century republic. When they are not, these archetypal realities should be illustrated at least by good drawings and paintings or appropriate photographs. For to deny our children familiarity with the experience shared by all times and all places is to deprive them further ecologically and culturally.

There are factual nuances, to be sure, of which children, as they mature, can be made aware: the "lilies of the field" probably were in fact scarlet anemones (since our lilies do not easily grow in Palestine and kings wore bright red-purple robes). Sheep are in fact dirty and stupid, need stones thrown at their thick pelts to guide them and songs sung to them for reassurance (which tells us much about how realistically our good shepherd Jesus assesses our frailty). In the Semitic East even today, a king sits in judgment with his courtiers roundabout, a scene which has produced in the Bible the constantly recurring picture and language of a formal law suit (in Hebrew, *rîb*) set in the court of God surrounded by the powerful lords of heaven (who include as prosecuting attorney the *satan* or "adversary" whose job is to bring out the worst in the case of the person under trial).

Such encyclopedic details can enrich our understanding of biblical imagery but are rarely essential for our understanding of the points that are usually made in universal terms.

Some archeological details can add color, such as the habit of some of the pharisees of inserting thorns into their garment hems to ward off the touches of the ritually impure. However, even if this custom is not generally known, the mingled hope and fear of the woman suffering from the flow of blood and Christ's loving power are clear enough.

4. *Parables*. How images teach more clearly than abstract statements can be seen especially in Jesus' stories. Here I would strongly urge the reader to search out and read *The Parables of Jesus* by the German scholar, J. Jeremias. Especially worthy of study is his chapter, "The Message of the Parables of Jesus."

5. *Song*. Although we have lost the melodies, the Bible is full of music of every sort. In the midst of stories we have snatches of old war songs, serenades, harvesters' chanties, and wedding dances as well as the recurring picture of men and women bursting into personal compositions expressing their joy or grief. Liturgical use is made of a vast variety of wind, string, and percussion instruments. Within the Bible's hymn book, many psalms are clearly borrowed from royal marches, caravan choruses, and even from folk melodies expressing the forbidden "pagan" mythology of the land of Canaan.

Songs are powerful and have toppled empires, set men free, and driven them mad. The eclecticism of the compilers of the psalms and the power and truthfulness of so much of the music in the life of the young today should encourage us to borrow freely for our liturgies—if the music is good and the words strong. Namby-pamby whining cannot give glory to God.

OURS TO ACCEPT

Eucharist is a word which at root level seems to mean: a graceful thing (*charis*—charm, gracefulness) well done (*eu*). "Efcharisto" as it is pronounced today is the usual way of saying "thank-you" in Greek. One hot Saturday morning a Cypriot boy taught me something of a deeper dimension within this concept during our excavations at an ancient copper trading site.

A kindly farmer had seen the two of us perspiring over plans and surveying instruments and was moved to bring us a little tray with two cool glasses of lemonade and a few salty Ritz crackers. After gratefully draining my glass I was trying politely to refuse the crackers by shaking my head and repeating the words *Efcharisto poli*—to mean "No, thank-you"—when I suddenly noticed my young assistant had become very upset and was trying to signal me secretly. As the farmer smilingly continued to offer the crackers and as I repeated my demurral, Stavros finally blurted out at me in his school English: "Take it— it is from the man." In that instant I abruptly realized that an integral part of a eucharistic exchange must be the *acceptance* of what is offered. Throughout all our lives, but especially within our eucharistic liturgies, we should both *acknowledge* God's kindness and *accept* what he is giving.

Ours to accept is his word: the good news, his most precious gift to us—our most precious gift to our children—to be passed on gracefully and well, with delight and truthfulness, so that it will come to pass that they go and do likewise.

This section was written by Father Carney E. S. Gavin, Assistant Curator of the Harvard Semitic Museum at Harvard University.

Discovering the Old Testament

Educating children is a serious matter—or do we take it too seriously? The confusion evident in that statement is genuine.

Many people believe that children must grow up. They can't remain naive children forever, they can't have everything they want, they have to begin to fit in, keep quiet, do the "right" things and avoid the "wrong" things, and so on. In other words, they must be educated, socialized—for their own "good" and, consequently, for their parents' and neighbors' good, for society's good, and so on. Sooner or later they must pass from childhood to "reality" if they are to survive along with the rest of us. For these people education, socialization is a *serious* matter. It prepares the child for adult life. Upon it hinges the child's material and psychic welfare.

But other people argue that an education that simply represses the playfulness and carelessness of childhood does serious damage to the child and society. It begets neurotic adults and maintains a neurotic society. They argue that human society as we experience it is basically a group-survival mechanism founded upon the uneasiness the individual feels before this mute, mysterious universe. Wouldn't it be better, they say, if we educated our children to a less anxious relationship to their world; if we educated them to life and not so much to mutual survival—allowing that there is an important difference between truly living and just surviving?

This is an important controversy to consider when discussing the use of the Old Testament in educating a child. The Hebrew Bible is an educational compendium; it is a teaching instrument, a volume of lessons collected over the centuries before Christ to develop the consciousness and behavior of Hebrew youth and adults. What was its intention—or the intention of its various parts? I think a thorough analysis of the Old Testament must lead one to conclude that it lines up with an educational philosophy that favors openness, spontaneity, courageous living, and stands opposed to an educational philosophy that stoically fosters repression, conformity and cautious or aggressive survival, and to the kinds of society begotten of such a philosophy. This is not to deny that the Old Testament has been used in the past to repress people, to preserve the arrangements and the class distinctions of societies, to encourage faithful soldiering, to justify the excommunication of social misfits, to support the ethic of, say, a passing economic or political system to the point where the Old Testament's own transcendent critique of all human civilizations and systems was betrayed.

But under the influence of the Spirit we have more access to the true biblical message and ethic today. We have a clearer understanding of the true educational intent of the biblical tradition and of the kind of human society it advocates—a society of freedom based on love and a profound sense of harmony with the universe; a sober society, fully aware of satanic forces that still generate fear, alienation and their psychic, intellectual and social consequences, yet a society unsubmissive and confident of victory in the face of them; a society we call "the People of God."

FEAR OR FAITH?

In Genesis 11 we have the story of the Tower of Babel. It expresses the Bible's attitude toward man-made civilizations. People come together. Alone they feel helpless before nature; life is a hardship. But together they begin to master their environment, build up their sense of security, pass from newfound courage to arrogance, and move on to extend their dominion indefinitely. They build a tower "whose top shall reach the heavens."

But fear was the foundation of those magnificent, impressive empires; fear maintained them and their apparent unity was undermined by fear. No one really understood or trusted his neighbor. The social systems set up by man failed to resolve man's fear, man's sense of alienation in this world. Instead they tended to increase it.

Genesis goes on to tell the story of one man who left such a civilization, a man who was educated to a better solution to his fears. The man was Abraham, and his educational journey carried him to intimate union with the source of the universe and to the fullness of life. Abraham is the father of "the People of God"—a society that emulates his faith and transcends and opposes all human systems that are based on fear, maintained by fear and are content with material goals and a modicum of life.

The Christian who uses the Old Testament as an educational resource must be aware of its true values and liberating thrust; must use it to **salvage child-hood** openness and spontaneity while, at the same time, equipping the **child** with an ability not simply to conform to the standards of the current culture, but to judge that culture by the standards of God and God's heroes—by the standards of the child's true and eternal society, the People of God. Once this is clear, the Bible is wide open to effective, intelligent use by a parent or teacher.

TELL IT IN EPISODES

Nor is there any need to be systematic about its use—especially with children. Children tend to be satisfied with episodes. They tend to be impatient with long stories and historical surveys. They may indeed want to hear the *whole* life story of a David or Moses or Daniel Boone, but even then, they like it in discrete episodes—without concern for chronology. An Alpha to Omega treatment of salvation history should be reserved until adolescence when the need for comprehensive understanding will be greater.

The Bible lends itself to piecemeal use. Most of the books are compilations of pre-existing stories, oracles, sayings and prayers. For instance, the book of Genesis gathers together several brief stories about Abraham that probably were told in isolation, like the stories we used to hear about George Washington and the cherry tree and Abraham Lincoln's wrestling with Jack Armstrong.

In the biblical Abraham's case we have the story of his trip to Egypt and the problem he experienced there (Gn 12:10-20). We have two other versions of that same story later on (Gn 20:1-18; 26:6-11), the apparition by the terebinth at Mamre (Gn 18:1-15), the sacrifice of Isaac (Gn 22:1-19). In Genesis these stories have been drawn out of the isolation of oral tradition and linked editorially; they have been made the building blocks of a complete Abraham legend serving the theme of his extraordinary faith.

The same is true of most of Genesis. The creation stories, the stories of Cain and Abel, Noah, the Tower of Babel, the episodes we read about Jacob and his sons pre-existed the book we call Genesis and still retain their particular outlines and unity, even though they are now made to serve the larger purposes of the compilers.

THE SPIRIT OF MOSES

The same is true of that whole "shelf" of books: Josue, Judges, 1 and 2 Samuel and 1 and 2 Kings. Those books all come out of one great literary effort. Back around 620 B.C. roughly, when the kingdom of Judah was all that was left of the once great kingdom of David and Solomon, prophetic writers decided that Judah needed to reform, get back to the spirit of Moses. They therefore put together the book of Deuteronomy in which Moses addresses the Israelites before they enter Palestine and lays down the law—emphasizing absolute fidelity to Yahweh, the only God, and avoidance of any temptation to slip into the attractive but myopic, superstitious, materialistic and therefore repressed cultures of the world.

To back up the book of Deuteronomy with illustrations they then put together a whole history of Israel from the time of Josue's conquest and the tribal years (c. 1200-1000 B.C.) through the years of great glory and prosperity under David and Solomon (c. 1000-922 B.C.) and thence into the troubled years of division and decline leading down to c. 620 B.C., the time of the composers of this historical work. The purpose of the long history of Josue, Judges, 1 and 2 Samuel and 1 and 2 Kings is to show how whenever Israelite tribes or individuals remained pure, faithful to the spirit of Moses, they prospered; whenever they gave way to greed, the instinct to survive by power and deceit, whenever they lived purely by the principles of earthbound systems, they went under.

A rich variety of stories was available to the composers of these books— stories about Gideon, Ehud, Samson, Saul, David, the prophets Elijah and Elisha. They were well suited to convey the basic message of the reform writers about the consequences of fidelity and infidelity and so they were woven into the theme and emerge now as parts of that overall history.

Besides these large compilations of materials that are basically episodic there are other narrative pieces in the Old Testament like the books of Ruth and Esther and Judith that can appeal to children.

Stick with the narrative material we have helped you identify above. Generally speaking, the prophetic and wisdom literature will have less appeal to children (although Proverbs might be fun).

PARAPHRASE THE STORIES

How would one use this Old Testament narrative material? It wouldn't be wise to use the stories just as they are. Some are quite to the point, like the Cain and Abel story. But others are complicated, repetitious and contain references to ancient customs, conditions, and primitive moral codes that are distracting and require perhaps more explanation than they are worth—given our purpose in using the stories. So in most cases it is good to paraphrase the stories, streamline them, accentuate the main features and message. This is legitimate—but it requires a good understanding and assimilation of the stories by the adult who uses them. And that requires consultation of sound but popular exegetical works like the Paulist Press *Pamphlet Bible Series.*

Once one has a grasp of a story's message, one can simply tell it (paraphrasing it); tell it with illustrations; have children play it out; do it with puppets. Then draw out their questions and comments on the story. Help them translate their impressions into an abstract of the story's point and then immediately have them make simple applications of the point to situations in their own life. Don't relate them to situations bigger than their own—e.g., to the national political situation or crime or even to world peace or the problem of famine in some far off place. Limit the application to their immediate milieu, their limited experience—schoolyard situations, family situations, visible, experienced economic and social situations. In the course of time the child's horizons will widen and reference to his or her wider realm of experience can then be made. But by then perhaps the message of the story will be assimilated and the practice of its application made easy no matter what the circumstances as the child advances through life.

THE STORY OF SAMSON

Take the Samson cycle in Judges 13-16. This collection of episodes will indeed have to be simplified and paraphrased. But Samson is an attractive character. He illustrates an important but simple point: Do not succumb to the attraction of a culture whose standards fall short of love, respect for the dignity of every person, belief in a God who is bigger than nature, kings and cultures, yet personal, caring and insistent on creating a human society that embodies his personality and care.

"Do not succumb to the attractions of a culture whose standards fall short of love . . . "

Samson started out a firm believer in such a God and bore witness to that belief by opposing the aggressive, avaricious culture of the Philistines. He let his hair grow to show that he liked himself as God made him. He kept away from wine and strong drink because God's spirit was spirit enough for him. And because of his independence and higher values he was strong, vital. He made Philistines look puny and timid—although as a matter of fact it was their lack of faith and hope and genuine love that made them puny and timid.

But Samson compromised himself. The Philistine public relations people got the best of him. He really began to think that "Coke was the real thing," that General Mills and Mattell and the Mayor of Gaza had all our interests at heart. Delilah, whose name reflects the Hebrew word for "night," clipped his free-flowing hair, that symbol of his independence and pure relation to the personal, caring God of Israel.

By relaxing his convictions, his faith, Samson lost his power and attractiveness. By succumbing to Philistine influences he became weak, puny, a slave; he lost his vision; he walked in circles at a hand-mill, going nowhere—all characteristics of people who fail to live affirmative, courageous, genuinely open and loving lives. Of course, Samson regains his faith and strength and at least brings down the system that enslaved him. A not too constructive result to a tragic career. But one can learn from Samson.

THE WAY TO MATURITY

With some thought and imagination, with some dramatization and illustrations this narrative can engage children and find application to their own lives and situations. The risk, of course, is that they may grow up independent, critical of their surroundings by God's standards and a bit too free and creative for whatever Philistine forces may still be with us. But then, we said at the beginning that biblical education does not intend to turn youth into anonymous, "well behaved," conformist, polarized adults. It does not really lend itself to an educational philosophy that produces that kind of adult. It does not suppress childhood openness, ambition, spontaneity, a sense of harmony with nature (Jesus said: Unless you become as little children you will never enter the kingdom of heaven). But it does add two things to that openness and harmony, to the virtues of childhood.

They are, *first*, awareness of the satanic, awareness of a real force affecting all of us and summoning us to recoil from life and love for survival's sake, a cringing force that shrivels things up (like the Wicked Witch of the West in the *Wizard of Oz*), a backward, a regressive force that is ultimately attracted to the womb and the tomb. Psychologists have called it the death instinct.

And *second*, the courage and faith to oppose that force in oneself and in the world for God's sake and the sake of the good world and good society outlined in Genesis 1-2.

A blend of childhood freedom, openness, playfulness plus a courageous awareness of sin and readiness for a struggle that must issue in victory—this blend makes for true maturity. And this is what the Bible teaches. This is what biblical narratives about Samson, Abraham, Josue, Gideon, Saul, David and the rest can ultimately convey.

Geoffrey Wood, author of this section, did graduate study and extensive teaching in Old and New Testament literature. He holds a licentiate in biblical studies and a doctorate in biblical theology. He lives in Sonoma, California, where he is a management consultant and a program evaluator in human services.

Discovering the New Testament

The New Testament is a book of the church and children belong to the church. Therefore it is their book. As they grow up in the church it is going to be shared with them on some terms. The concern of the authors of this volume is that it be shared with them on good terms.

The New Testament, like the bulk of the Hebrew Bible on which it is based, is a book of stories. There are exceptions to this rule in both instances. In the Christian scriptures there is little legal writing and only a certain amount of proverbial writing, most of it found on the lips of Jesus. A large part of New Testament moral exhortation, at least as regards its form, and the theological probing of the epistles of Paul (and the epistle to the Hebrews) are matters to which the Jewish collection is a stranger. By and large, however, the 27 books in the Christian canon are made up of stories: tales which Jesus told, tales told about him, tales of the journeyings of the early Christians, some of them by Paul about himself in his letters. The stories were told as part of the effort to spread the good news that God is love and, in the case of the disciples' preaching, that Jesus is Lord.

As a general rule stories are interesting. Some, of course, can be boring. The point of a story remains in memory if the tale is told well. The task of the teacher of children is to master the best of the New Testament's stories and tell them well.

THE CENTRAL STORY

The central story of the New Testament is about a young Jewish man who loved his people and lived their life. He tried to help them fulfill their hopes and dreams by turning their thoughts continually to God and his love. He succeeded with some, he did not succeed with others. When the occupying power in his country executed him on suspicion of fomenting political upheaval, he died bravely with forgiveness on his lips. For his total fidelity and obedience to the God of Israel, whom he called "my Father," he was raised from the dead. The upraising of all faithful Jews at the last day was thus anticipated in the person of Jesus. He was hailed by those who believed in him as the first-fruits of a harvest to come. This was their way of expressing their faith that what God meant to do for all he had first done for his son Jesus.

It is very important for anyone who plans children's liturgies to master the central story that developed into Christianity. Just as there is no Jewish existence without the story of the deliverance from Egypt on the night of the first Passover, so there is no Christian existence without a mastery of Christian beginnings. The account of Jesus' death and resurrection is first in importance of all the New Testament narratives. The song sung over the Easter candle at the night vigil is a good summary of the story of our salvation as it is found in the Bible. Like most stories, it is better sung than spoken. Dividing it up to be spoken in parts is a good plan but doing the same with the "trial" or passion narratives is a bad one. That helps people forget where the real guilt lies.

Second after this story in importance comes that of the birth of the community of believers on the day of Pentecost. The third Christian story—that of Jesus' birth as we have it from Luke and Matthew—is a very attractive one. It is not a little puzzling, being concerned, especially in Matthew, with the child's possible illegitimacy. We may not forget the important fact that the two evangelists were not interested in his babyhood or his helplessness. They told a tale about the beginnings of the existence of this child in order to underscore the power that would be his as a grown man. The nativity story, like all good stories for children, is essentially about the loss of the limitations of childhood.

The planner of children's celebrations will do as much study of the central story of the New Testament as (s)he can, remembering that Paul's preaching of it at the beginning of 1 Corinthians 15 is the basic statement. Another account of how our salvation was accomplished occurs in Acts 10:34-43. That summary is attributed to Peter but in fact was written by the author of Acts, the same person who wrote the gospel according to Luke. He has a theory of the transmission of chosen peoplehood from the Jews to the Gentiles which we are not wise to follow too closely (verses 39 and 40, for example). But we can profit by his telling of the central tale of salvation both here and elsewhere (e.g., in Acts 2:22-36; 4:8-12; 13:26-39, the latter a sermon attributed to Paul but identical in spirit with the sermons of Peter).

TELLING TALES

The story of our salvation is a myth. This technical literary term means that it is true but is such in a way too large for our comprehension. Its mythical form makes it easy to tell and easy for the hearer of good will to receive. We speak of the story as too large to take in because it is a tale of good and evil in conflict, of God and his love for us versus all that is mean and selfish in the world ("the devil and his power"), of God's acceptance of the death of a good man and the application of the human goodness of this one man to all others.

No one can understand a proposed explanation of the totality of life which has as much sweep as that, not even the keenest saint or theologian. The only way to transmit and receive it is by way of a story, and that is the way it came to us. Jesus knew that if people were to believe in his Father as he asked them to they had to become like little children. They had to cry out: "Tell us a story." He said once in a prayer: "Father . . . what you have hidden from the learned and the clever you have revealed to the merest children" (Matthew 11:25). That is our charter for storytelling. It is impossible to believe in Christianity on any other terms than to accept it in childlike faith as a story.

There is a lot of Jewish mythology in the New Testament that the storyteller cannot hope to come abreast of all at once, perhaps ever. There is no need to do so. With time, that which is essential in the world of biblical imagination can be mastered. That means that one does not worry about explaining every bloc of symbols one encounters in the New Testament, least of all attempt to solve matters by explaining symbols away. One tells the story as soon as one can find the words to do so.

"But later they will grow up to discover that the stories weren't true, just as they learn about Santa Claus and the Easter Bunny, and they will feel that religion was part of a great deceit called childhood!"

That will be so only if there is an unwise selection of tales with emphasis on all the wrong elements—a religion, for example, that features the Gadarene swine and Ananias and Sapphira and Judas's entrails spilling out. One can even tell the great mystery of our faith in topsy-turvy fashion, with God threatening and punishing everyone and the demons having as prominent a place in the story of salvation as Jesus. That is possible and we have to admit it. It has happened before and will probably happen again. But anyone in the church who hopes to pass the faith along must master the great central story and tell it well, even while running all the attendant risks. That story is true. It has to be told.

NO TIME FOR BANALITY

We are witnessing in our day an adult rejection of Christianity by people who are discovering American Indian religion, Buddhist mythology, the *Iliad* and the *Odyssey*, the epic of Cuchulainn, astrology, tarot cards, Sufi mysticism. What can that mean if not that a hunger of the heart for great stories told well is a key to the mystery of life? How explain it but as a refusal of thin gruel, namely our Christian faith, which is one of the world's great religious epics, turned into a banal moralism?

Jesus had no time for banality. He told great tales. That is chiefly what he did when he taught. Whoever passes his teaching along must master his stories. They are of two kinds chiefly, the great parables of mercy found in Luke and the reign-of-God parables found in Matthew and Mark. The parables of the second type feature two basic alternatives and ask the hearer to choose. The key to Jesus' stories—and they are not easy to interpret just because they are not banal—is that God does not see life the way we do. He has a different scheme of values and will turn things upside down in the end. The wisest choice we can make is to opt for turning them upside down now—to get on his wavelength before it is too late. Such is the deepest meaning of Jesus' parables.

There is one large hazard in telling our Lord's stories which must be avoided at all cost. Not even the gospel writers managed to stay entirely clear of it. It is the temptation to turn them into petty moralities, tales of "good guys" and "bad guys" of a kind he had absolutely no interest in. To do that is to miss the point. The point of his stories is that there is a fundamental option in life. "What do you wish to make of yourself now that you're here? You can't sneak out. There's no running away. Will you submit to God's rule over you or will you try to run your own show?" That is the underlying question in Jesus' kingdom parables. An adult cannot spend too much time studying all about the parables so as to tell them well and not ruin them by "explanations" that miss the thrust of Jesus' teaching.

MIRACLES AND MARVELS

There are a couple of pitfalls to avoid in teaching *about* Jesus, assuming that teaching the things he taught—including his splendid wisdom in proverbs—will be done well. One is to fear teaching the wondrous aspects of this man we call our Savior. The other is to teach his wondrous aspects in a way that is heretical—a departure from the basics of Catholic Christianity. A modern, thoughtful transmitter of the Christian story might easily fall into the first pitfall as a result of efforts to avoid the second. So many of today's adults were taught about Jesus badly—his human character and insights deemphasized, his divine character stressed to the near obliteration of his humanity and Jewishness—that they are prone to make new errors in their efforts to set the balance right. They might hesitate, for example, to feature the multiplication of the loaves, the stilling of the storm, the resuscitation of Lazarus—all because as children they were subjected to a pulpit christology that featured very little else. But any such muting of the miraculous, the marvelous in the life of Jesus would be a great mistake. It would be to disarm the apostolic teachers in their efforts to show that in this man the normal limitations of humanity did not apply. It would be to rob children of the rich symbol of power used for the sake of goodness: a power they do not have, an adult goodness they are constantly charged with not possessing.

Many modern parents have been silent with their children about the gospel portrait of Jesus "until they can understand." They then learn with shock and surprise that Superman has invaded their totally rational household with a vengeance. The child cannot do without a world of marvel and surprise. If one has not been proposed it will be invented. The gospels present a Jesus who acts in the power of the Spirit because he is a prayerful and trusting son. It is a blunder to minimize his works of power for fear that much that is taught now will have to be retracted later. If it is taught well, nothing will have to be retracted later. The child is not put off by power but rather revels in it and asks for more.

Teaching Jesus' works of power *badly* is the threat to later faith. The way this is usually done is to present him as God in a human space-suit on a walk in space. The notion is heretical, of course. The New Testament will not countenance it. Yet it has a very lively history and probably a lively future. Readers of this book are invited in the name of God to have nothing to do with it. The main form it takes is attributing to Jesus in his lifetime full knowledge of everything that ever happened plus the absolute power of God himself; put crassly, an awareness at all times that, "I am God." This presentation is separated by a world from the picture painted of him in the New Testament books. There he is a Jewish man who has a great mission, a son of God who does all that the Father expects of him and who is glorified for it as *the* son of God. He is intimate with God in a unique way. He is someone who possesses a total self-confidence with no admixture of repentance or regret. Even when the evangelists and other writers work out theories of Jesus' closeness to God, they do it in terms of the immediate presence of God's Word or Wisdom or Spirit to this man. Jesus is never "merely a man" in the New Testament. He is a man so suffused with the Spirit of God that it is right to call him a divine person. But a divine person is not necessarily an offspring of the Father who is using a non-personal "humanity" as his instrument, despite the popularity of this theological explanation. There are other possibilities. The obvious one is that the "one person" of the Christian creeds is Jesus of Nazareth. The New Testament knows nothing of a "humanity" being used from inside, as it were, by God or the Word of God. It reports only on a man before God who is conscious of a unique closeness to him, a perfect trust, and the certainty that God will respond fittingly to this trust which Jesus reposes in him. He is unequivocally, as the New Testament calls him, the only son of God.

PAUL, HEBREWS, AND ACTS

The teacher needs to study with great care Paul's telling of the Christ story. Paul has no interest in the Jesus story of the gospels. He tells a story of "Jesus now" and the only Jesus there is now is Jesus Christ, Lord, Redeemer, Savior. In none of this glorification has his sharing of our human lot been lost. He continues to do things for us because he is one of us. His being with the Father in glory has not diminished his interest in us, it has heightened it. Such is St. Paul's conviction.

The anonymous Epistle to the Hebrews is even better than Paul, in a way, at conveying the reality of a Jesus who at every moment is with us and for us. The setting chosen is culturally somewhat foreign to us, namely the ritual behavior of Jewish priests engaged in temple sacrifice. But the message of Hebrews cannot be lost. Jesus felt the mental anguish of being human and being abandoned. He gave his life for his sisters and brothers whom he represented to the full. He could do this because he was one with them in every respect. It is important to master the story of Jesus' service to us as a brother which the Epistle to the Hebrews tells particularly well.

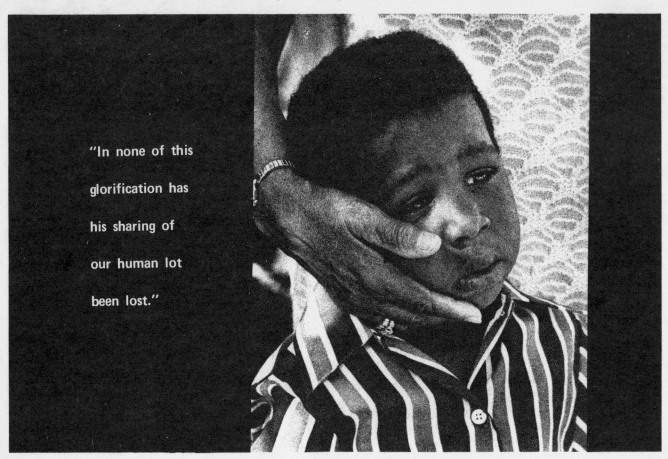

"In none of this glorification has his sharing of our human lot been lost."

The book of the Acts of the Apostles needs to be used with special care, the more especially as its stories are so vivid and so gripping. Think, for example, of the tales of sharing of the early Jerusalem community, of Paul's journeys, of his shipwreck and being worshiped on the sands of Malta as a god. The account of Paul in Acts is done from sources with a lively dose of theological presupposition added, much of it non-Pauline. This means that Paul himself is more trustworthy on Paul than Acts is. Read, for example, the first two chapters of Galatians or much of 2 Corinthians and all of Philemon to learn what his adventures were and how he thought about things. Above all, don't take Romans 7:13-25 as autobiographical because it isn't. Paul worried a lot about a theological concept which he personified as Sin, but scarcely ever about *his* sins. He seemed to regret only one thing, having persecuted the church of God. For the rest, he had a very robust conscience. He was not an introspective man who "pulled himself apart." Quite the contrary. He was marvelously at ease over his own chances at salvation because of his total faith in Christ and the power of God.

POETRY AND TRUTH

There is no end to the study of the New Testament that the creator of liturgies for children can profitably engage in. More important than studying it, though, is reading it, believing it, savoring it. The New Testament is true in all that it tells us in the way that good poetry is true, in the way that an epic masterpiece is true. Its books are a proclamation of Jesus Christ and he is God's truth. Their rich Jewish symbolism, a storehouse of images, is the gift to us of the Spirit of truth.

If anyone says, "Well you can't be satisfied sharing images with children, just filling their heads with symbols; you have to teach them the truth," that person can never learn anything from the Bible. As for "truth," what a dreary and distorted and downright misleading business it is bound to be in the hands of such a one. (S)he wouldn't be comfortable for five minutes in the company of our blessed Lord or St. Paul or even that magnificent mad artist who threw paint everywhere but on the canvas, the author of Jude.

This section was written by Gerard S. Sloyan, a priest of Trenton, New Jersey. He is a professor of religion at Temple University in Philadelphia and chairperson of the board of directors of the Liturgical Conference.

A Book for Common Prayer

The Bible does not live a life of its own. It came into being and continues to exist only in relationship to a worshiping community. An individual can study and meditate upon its words to his great benefit, but the truest framework for the Bible, the situation in which it is most itself, is the liturgical celebration. Indeed many parts of the Bible originated in a liturgical setting, and can only be fully understood by those who have experienced that setting themselves. Who, for example, can truly understand the gospel accounts of the last supper if (s)he has not participated in the Christian eucharist? Can a person understand the account of the Exodus who has not shared the passover meal with believing Jews? Or, conversely, can anyone see more than a "nice custom" in the passover meal who has not read the stirring biblical account of Moses and his erstwhile loyal band? The Bible is an account of the religious experience of a community; it was written by and is best understood by that believing community, and we become that community in the liturgical assembly.

Certainly religious groups can and do offer genuine worship without reference to the Bible. For Christians, however, this is not possible because revelation, the presence and power of God through his word, is at the very center of belief. Scripture is part of the definition of the relationship between the Christian people and their God.

You might say that liturgy is a door and scripture the key which unlocks that door. It does not merely describe and define, but draws the community into the religious event. This close relationship between scripture and worship becomes more and more obvious to those who are engaged in the planning of liturgies. The scripture readings give form and fabric to the celebration much as yeast gives body and texture to bread. The creator of children's liturgies, then, must take the selection of scripture very seriously. The readings or psalms must establish a mood or theme, focus attention, engage the minds and emotions of the participants, point to and clarify the actions of celebrant and congregation.

Good treatment of the scriptural element of a liturgy is as important as good selection. The aim of the liturgy is, after all, to celebrate, not to explain; to draw together or explore, but not to expound. Often, when the scripture passage is "weak," unrelated to the theme, or when there is no coordination between scripture and a clarifying ritual, then the homilist carries the whole burden of "pulling off" the liturgy. He ends by teaching rather than preaching, or by offering some reflections to the children on a totally unrelated subject.

How then can we develop children's liturgies in such a way that scripture and ritual action complement, explain and reinforce one another? Here are some guidelines which this close relationship between scripture and liturgy suggests.

1. SELECT A THEME

The process of selection really begins before any of your resource books are consulted, when the question is asked, "What are we going to celebrate?" The answer may be "joy at being alive," or "baptism" or "the Bicentennial" or "sunshine" or "the sense of touch," or "Mother's Day." An absolute essential in the selection of a children's liturgy theme is that it be as specific and concrete as possible. For example, young children might find "joy at being alive" too abstract to celebrate. In what ways are they *aware* of being alive? A child's name is a sign to him that he is someone; it identifies him to himself as well as to others, and is a more important sign of his aliveness than is his breathing. Thus a liturgy could be built around "names." Luke 2:21 (the naming of Jesus) and John 1:41-42 (the renaming of Peter) or any one of a number of name-changing scenes from scripture can be used. Along with one or two of these, Rv 2:17 could be used: "To the victor I will give the hidden manna; I will aso give him a white stone upon which is inscribed a new name, to be known only by him who receives it."

On some occasions, you will begin with a general topic, such as "giving thanks" and narrow it down only when you have found a good reading. Gn 1:26: "Let them have dominion over the fish of the sea, the birds of the air, and the cattle, and over all the wild animals and all the creatures that crawl on the ground," for example, might suggest a "liturgy of thanksgiving *for pets*." At other times you will have a very specific topic in mind before beginning the search. In September, when children are excited about their new clothes and lunchboxes and notebooks, they would respond well to a "liturgy of thanksgiving *for back-to-school things*." In this case a better reading would be Rv 21:1-6: "See, I make all things new!"

2. THINK OF THE MAIN READING AND RITUAL AS ONE

Once the theme is established and the main reading selected, a main action should be chosen. It is important to think of the keynote reading and ritual together, not that they will happen simultaneously, but so that they are integral and sharply focused. The liturgical action should seek to renew, for these children at this celebration, that religious experience which the scripture proclaims. The "liturgy of thanksgiving for pets" mentioned above, for example, could be held out-of-doors and include a procession and blessing of the pets; the "liturgy of thanksgiving for back-to-school things" could include a "blessing of the lunchboxes." In the case of the "celebration of names," the children could be given small white stones as they come forward to receive the eucharist (the hidden manna). Or, in a less literal visualization of the passage from Revelation, they could write their names boldly on a giant stone which would then be carried in procession to the altar, or could itself be used as the altar. This use of a single stone would be especially suitable early in the school year, when the children are just discovering that they are a community, as well as individuals.

In this process of designing the liturgy the children should of course be involved to whatever degree possible. It is more valuable to plan *with* the children, even if some of their ideas seem less than perfect, than to plan *for* them.

3. ADD SONGS, READINGS, AND RITUALS AS NEEDED

For example, the children could write new verses for Ps 148 (frogs and gerbils, praise the Lord) or for the hymn of the three young men (Dn 3:57ff.) to be sung during the pet procession. Other scripture verses can be used as meditations or responses, such as Ps 145:10-11: "Let all your works give you thanks, O Lord, and let your faithful ones bless you. Let them discourse of the glory of your kingdom and speak of your might." Non-scriptural readings should be considered also, of course (e.e. cummings—"I thank you God for most this amazing day").

We suggest thinking in terms of "keynote" and "supplemental" readings rather than "epistle" and "gospel" because each passage from scripture has its own flavor, or several levels of meaning, and it is distracting to try to give each one equal attention. Two readings on the same topic, in other words, might suggest different hymns or rituals or visual accompaniments. On the theme of "growing up" for example, Lk 2:51-52—"Jesus, for his part, progressed steadily in wisdom and age and grace before God and men"—suggests marking the children's increasing physical and mental growth in some way, perhaps with the use of posters and photographs showing how they have grown, learned more, developed since they were babies. On the other hand, another passage which speaks of growing up, Eph 4:11-16—"each has his own gift, but we all grow up in the one body of Christ"—suggests an emphasis on the unique gift or talent each child makes to the community. Still another passage from Ephesians (1:3-19), speaks of growing up in the spiritual gifts of faith and love, and suggests the relationship of growth to baptism. If it were used as the keynote reading, the liturgy might include a rite of baptismal renewal.

4. ADAPT THE SCRIPTURES TO THE CHILDREN

Ephesians 1:3-19, mentioned above, is a good illustration of this principle. These 16 verses are too long for most occasions. Verses 7 through 12 could be eliminated or the entire passage greatly simplified without any distortion to the meaning or cadence of the original. Verses 15 through 19 are a very warm and personal blessing from the author to the Christians of Ephesus whom he loved and depended upon. They would be a very suitable dismissal blessing at the end of the celebration. They could be dropped from the earlier reading or simply repeated as a blessing. The first and last lines will need tailoring so that sentences are not left dangling.

There are many forms of legitimate adaptation, such as dropping the jealous brother from the story of the prodigal to allow young children to concentrate on the relationship between father and younger son, or using contemporary money and measurements, or translating entire parables into modern language (a migrant farm worker was going from Jerusalem to Jericho when he fell among a band of grape growers . . .). When good judgment is exercised the authentic meaning can be enhanced, or the biblical ambience made more vivid. It is, however, never a good idea to "juice up" a story merely to add entertainment value (then the elephants came onto the ark, then the giraffes came onto the ark, then the kangaroos . . .) or to add on one's own moral lesson for the children (Jesus went down to Nazareth and lived under their authority and he helped with the dishes every night without complaining and studied his lessons very hard).

"each
has
his
own
gift . . . "

5. ADAPT THE THE RUBRICS ALSO

Besides adapting the language of scripture, it is also wise sometimes to make adaptations in the rubrics of the service—if it is a eucharist that is being celebrated. For example, the keynote reading may contain a phrase that can be used throughout the eucharist as a refrain ("Peace, be still." "Why search for the living among the dead?"). Therefore, a reading of that passage might be the very first event of the liturgy. On another occasion the use of five or six short readings might be more suitable than the standard epistle-gospel formula. The families might, for example, enter a darkened church, where they hear the sounds of voices arguing and gossiping, and angry shouts. Next they hear a reading on sin and ignorance such as Is 59:1-3, 7-11. Then comes a short interlude of recorded music (instrumental), a reading of Is 60:1-3—"Rise up in splendor! Your light has come"—the lighting of a large candle, accompanied by a reading of Jn 8:12— "I am the light of the world"—and finally Col 1:10-14—"He rescued us from the power of darkness." At this time the president of the assembly, with a very few words, should call the congregation to a silent consideration of their failures, and invite them to join in a confession of sin, after which each member of the congregation lights a taper from the large candle and gathers around the altar where the bread and wine are waiting.

In the liturgy just described the entire mass of the faithful has been reduced to the penitential rite, which has thus been highlighted. The four readings explain each other, proclaim the gospel of Jesus Christ, and draw the listeners into participation in the event. As in all good liturgy, they not only provide a motive for prayer, but the words for prayer as well.

6. THINK BEYOND "BIBLE STORIES"

You may have noted that all the examples of scripture used so far in this essay have been "theological" passages rather than parables, miracles, or events from the life of Jesus or another biblical personage. This was done for two reasons. In the first place, it is much less difficult to weave a good liturgy around a biblical passage that tells a story than to do the same thing with a passage that has no dramatic element. The story of the prodigal son, for example, can be told while appropriate modern photographs of boys and fathers are projected on a large screen, but what can be done with the writings of St. Paul? One could perhaps write "LOVE IS . . . " on a giant white piece of paper or cloth and invite the children to cover it with words that complete the sentence. This graffiti-sheet can then be used as an altar cloth or wall hanging, and 1 Cor 13: 4ff.—" . . . love is patient; love is kind. Love is not jealous . . . "—can be read.

Secondly, the stories of scripture will certainly play a large role in children's liturgies as they do in religious education. They are captivating and, because of their concrete imagery, lend themselves readily to dramatization, artistic representation, interpretation in song, and explanation through ritual. It must be remembered, though, that each story or event in the Bible is there to serve a religious purpose, to carry a message. For example, when we hear that Jesus calmed the storm it is not so that we can know Jesus as the super weather man, but so that we will know that he is with us and alert to the storms that beset us (Our God neither slumbers nor sleeps), and that his word to us is "peace" and "have faith." These meanings need not always be elaborated for the children. It is more important that the liturgist thoroughly understand them so that (s)he will be able to tell the story so well that the word will sink down into the hearts of the children.

7. LET THE IMAGES DO THEIR SHARE OF THE WORK

The Bible is filled with images, some immediately recognizable and understood, such as the sacred meal or fire. These are easy to use and frequently called forth during the liturgical year. The only danger here is one of staleness through over-use or unimaginative repetition. Others are more subtle, such as the tent, the journey to Jerusalem, or the breath of God. These require more creativity in their use in liturgy, but provide a treasure house of fresh ideas.

Go to a park, for example, and let all the children help to set aside or create a "sacred space" for their celebration. They can string clothesline among the trees and hang banners up, they can drape a colorful cloth over a picnic table and bring it into their enclosure. They can find wildflowers and pods to decorate it. Then, with a reading of Ex 3:1-6 (the burning bush), the presider can lead the children in taking off their shoes and socks as a sign of the holiness of the place where God and his people assemble, and they can help him "consecrate" the space with much holy water and incense, as a sign of the sacredness of the spot and the holiness of God. Very little verbal explanation should be necessary—the signs plus the reading from Exodus should be allowed to do their own "talking."

8. BE RELEVANT AND REALISTIC

The word "relevance" is somewhat discredited these days, and may conjure up images of dragging young children around to demonstrations and rallies. However, it does remind us that we must think first about what the children are really like, what experiences they have had, what their genuine response will be, and not what we can program it to be. In other words, let us design liturgies that examine the propensity of people to quarrel (see 1 Cor 1:10) or to feel jealousy (see the brother of the prodigal or the workers who spent the whole day in the field and got the same pay as those who only worked an hour), rather than endlessly celebrating the great togetherness we feel at being one big family of God. Children do not always behave perfectly, and they have fears and anxieties. These negative realities need to find expression in liturgy, as they have found expression in the Bible.

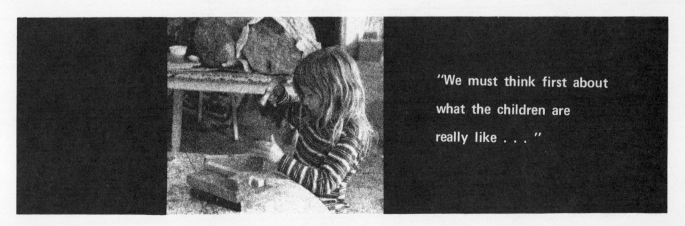

"We must think first about what the children are really like . . ."

9. BUT DON'T FORGET THE SIMPLICITY OF CHILDREN

Children do not share the adult need to celebrate only what is logical or profound. They can simply rejoice in the rain (see Ps 147:7-9), or in their ability to play a musical instrument (see Ps 150, Ps 98:5-8), or in their birthday (Job 10:11-12, Ps 8:4-9, Ps 139:13-17). These subjects can be fittingly celebrated in liturgy as long as adults do not treat them in a patronizing manner.

10. LET THE BIBLE TAKE THE SPOTLIGHT

The liturgy should help the children discover that the Bible is the source of the living word. The uniqueness of the book can be acknowledged, and a lasting impression made on the children without creating an atmosphere of hocus-pocus. Some techniques to consider are: choose good lectors and coach them in advance; give the lectors stoles; use a good translation or paraphrase; wait for silence and attention before reading; use colorful and appropriate covers for the Bible (macramé, needlework, burlap and felt—preferably made by the children themselves); include a variety of signs of reverence in your liturgies, such as processions with the book, incensing, kissing the book, placing the book on each child's head as a blessing. It is also a good idea to plan occasional liturgies on the theme of the Bible itself.

11. COLLECT RESOURCES

There is no easy way to find the "perfect" passage for a given celebration, but there are many resources to help in the search. The first and most essential resource is, of course, your own knowledge of scripture, and then whatever course notes, reference books, Bible concordances and indices you can gather. There are also a number of books available which give sample liturgies or collections of readings on a theme. However, these books can only give suggestions and useful combinations—they cannot provide liturgies ready-made for your children and situation.

Other useful sources for readings will be: prescribed readings of the three-year liturgical cycle, scriptural passages from the children's catechism books/lessons, suggestions by the children, the occasion of the celebration (beginning of school, birthday, solemn communion), or even the site of the liturgy (in the cafeteria, on a mountain, at grandmother's house). You may find it useful to keep a file of mimeographed papers from liturgies or Bible services, lists of favorite passages or interesting readings you discovered while looking for something else (always with the source noted so that you can find them again), lists and bibliographies from various sources. Religious education coordinators and liturgy directors usually maintain such files for the use of all teachers and liturgists in the parish.

This section was written by Elizabeth McMahon Jeep, editor of the revised edition of grades 1-4 of the Life, Love, Joy *catechetical series (Silver Burdett) and co-author of* Celebrate Summer *(Paulist Press). Exchange (Pflaum) is the best from the past five years of her column in* The Catechist.

Children
At Common
Prayer

Celebrating the Eucharist

In the deepest sense, the celebration of the eucharist is an adult activity, for through the eucharist the church manifests its share in the death and resurrection of Christ. Through Christ, with Christ, and in Christ, it offers praise and thanksgiving to the Father. Through him, with him, and in him, it says yes to God's purpose for mankind, accepting the wonder of the created world and human inventiveness and skill which are part of that world, facing the evil in the world and trusting that at last all things will be shaped to perfection under the loving hand of God. It is a yes to the share in Christ's cross which must fall upon all of us as we face sickness, death, disappointment, failure, and our own sinfulness. And it is a yes to bearing that cross by doing our share in building the kind of world that God wants. It is, above all, an expression of the faith that Christ's resurrection-triumph over sin and death is lasting and final, and that the beauty and good of this world will be brought to completion in him.

Children can and ought to participate in the eucharist for the same reason that we can repeat the eucharist again and again: we are, according to the gospels, all children before God, who only grow gradually into the maturity which is being a Christian, and which is the work of a lifetime. Christian worship knows no barriers of age because the requirements of Christian life are not a particular kind of knowledge or understanding, but an ability to respond with generosity and trust according to one's capacity for understanding. The ministry of Jesus manifests this attitude in the numerous rebukes to disciples who wanted to keep children away from him. Pope Paul VI, who embraces children when they bring gifts to the altar, and who pats them on the head at holy communion, reflects the same attitude.

REVERENCE OR REPRESSION?

One of the greatest barriers to the participation of children in the liturgy is not its formal ceremonial, but the attitudes and postures which adults bring to the ceremonial. Reverence is defined in an exclusively adult way, meaning a silent hush and the complete avoidance of natural gestures (e.g., smiling at somebody who is suddenly recognized halfway through mass). Children are felt to be a disruption if they bang kneelers or raise their voices to play with echoes in the large space of the building or wander into the aisle. It is objected that children are a distraction to prayer. Those who do not behave as little adults are removed or punished.

There are two questions which must be asked: Who is being distracted? and, What does reverence at the liturgy mean?

1. *Who is being distracted?* Children are expected to behave in church in a way that we do not expect them to behave at any other activity in which they are included. The fussiest of maiden aunts expects less of them than the average congregation. Anyone who has worked with teen-agers knows how hostile they often can be to organized religion, especially because it is perceived as repressive and unnatural. It is difficult to communicate to them that the church proclaims a loving and forgiving God, and equally difficult for them to believe that the church has any place for natural feelings and aspirations. Much of this, of course, has been subtly communicated by parents and teachers who believe that religion should be repressive and unnatural. But much of it, too, can be laid squarely at the door of organized religion which presents itself to them in its central act of worship as having no place for the feelings of children. The feeling that religion is unnatural is reinforced by countless childhood Sundays of being hushed and confined.

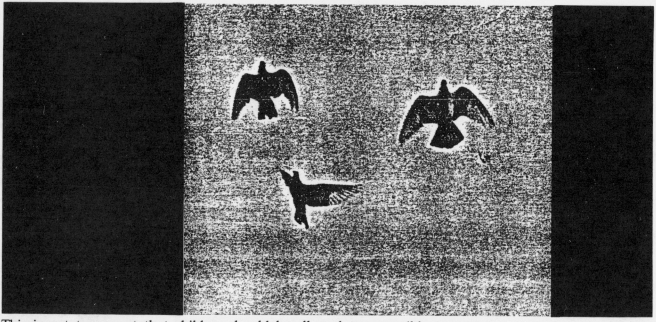

This is not to suggest that children should be allowed to run wild at mass. But any parent who is able to discipline (not repress) children effectively knows that they will respond well to certain expectations as long as they have enough freedom to move. For example, if children could be freer in their movements, they are apt to be able to be quieter, just as they can be still for a homily if they know they can relax a bit during the preparation of the altar and the gifts. If parents are not able to handle children in this way, perhaps the parish is not offering a kind of help outside of church that it should be.

2. *What does reverence at the liturgy mean?* One of the things which we often fail to take seriously is that the word, liturgy, means *public service*. It is primarily a sacred *action* in which we take part, not a devotion or a lesson.

The gospel writers emphasize this point by placing the eucharist not only in the setting of the last supper, but also in such events as the feeding of the multitude. The eucharist is a public action in the sense that it is an action in which all kinds and ages of people take part, each in their own way. Children's capacity for attention will inevitably be shorter than that of adults, and they should be expected to behave accordingly. It should be no source of dismay if they are inattentive to large portions of the prayers, the readings, and the homily. They will be there again, and we have a repeatable liturgy on the very human assumption that nobody gets it all in for once and for all at a single hearing.

Silence plays an important role in the liturgy, but small spaces of silence before prayers are likely to be as moving and significant for children as for adults. If there is to be a silence during the preparation of the altar and the gifts, it may be helpful to keep in mind that it is the silence of our own hearts which really counts, and soft instrumental music will not only cover most interruptions, but also quiet the people who are making the interruptions.

There are, of course, many who prefer a quiet devotional atmosphere. It must be firmly but gently taught (not just mentioned now and again) that the mass is not primarily a quiet devotional affair, but a public act. Parishes fail in their duty to meet the needs of the people by curtailing quiet devotional services at times other than mass for those who wish to have them. Many of our parochial problems could be met if we did such simple things as have teen-agers provide transportation and protection for older people who are afraid to come to evening services.

COMMUNICATING THROUGH GESTURE

Reverence at the liturgy is communicated less by silence than by ceremonial action. Unhurried and graceful gesture on the part of the ministers, and the vividness of such things as the smoke of incense, the use of bread that looks like bread, and communion from the chalice are all too frequently omitted or embarrassedly underplayed and diminished. Such things not only communicate a sense of reverence to older people; they do it for children as well. Nothing is more fascinating to a child than the smoke of incense or hands uplifted in prayer. Remembering the sterile rubricism that hurried or fussed over such things, we do not allow them to unfold for ourselves and our children. Because of our passion to answer the question, what does it mean?, we cut out all possibility of meaning. Many of these gestures only mean that we think we're doing something important, and that's enough. Nobody asks what it means to have fine china when you have company, or what it means to dress up in a suit and tie to go out for dinner.

In a variety of ways, we have discouraged and inhibited the use of lay people's gesture in the new liturgy (a development not envisaged by the liturgical books). Signs of the cross, kneeling (at least for short periods), beating the breast, bowing, genuflection, are all part of a heritage which has virtually disappeared. A real polemic was even launched against beating the breast—and it is the one gesture Jesus explicitly approves in the gospels, in the story of the Pharisee and the tax collector. The liturgy will be fit neither for children nor for adults unless these gestures are encouraged and developed. In a worship situation where the body was disliked less, it would probably even be possible to encourage the congregation to lift its arms in prayer with the priest—one of the most ancient of all Christian prayer postures.

A LITURGY FIT FOR EVERYBODY

Our first task is not to tailor the liturgy to fit children, but to develop it in such a way that it is fit, not only for children, but for everybody, to engage in a kind of worship which is truly catholic—a liturgy which worships with the body as well as with the mind, a liturgy which respects ceremonial as it respects word and music.

It should also be kept firmly in mind that the catechesis of children is primarily the responsibility of parents, and is primarily communicated in their own patterns of living and acting outside of church. The liturgy should never be used as a substitute for Christian life outside of public worship. The religious attitudes of parents will inevitably be communicated to their children, for good or ill. Often, the real need is not to provide a "message" for children, but to help parents be that message in their ordinary lives.

Nor need we be worried if children do not understand their faith in the same way adults do; children, after all, are children. Liturgy for children is not a matter of tailoring the worship of the church down to the child's level, but of having a kind of worship into which all can enter comfortably in their own way.

The ordinary Sunday liturgy for children, then, should be the ordinary parish mass, celebrated with dignity and care, but by people who are actually responsive to the needs of children among them, and in a way that allows children to enter as they can and will—in song, gesture, silence, and hearing as they are able.

An occasional parish mass which is more specifically oriented to the needs and desires of other groups would be helpful, even on a Sunday. Care should be taken not to do this on Sundays which are great "hinges" of the liturgical year, e.g., the First Sunday of Advent, Christmas, the First Sunday of Lent, Easter, or Pentecost. These are occasions of special significance for the whole church, and to have them specially adapted for a single group is to lose something of their immense significance for everyone. On the other hand, a Sunday within the seasons of Advent, Christmas, or Lent or the Easter season, might well be set aside with a special adaptation to families with children.

This section was written by Ralph Keifer, Associate Professor of Liturgy at St. Mary's Seminary in Baltimore. Married and the father of three, Dr. Keifer holds a Ph.D. in theology from Notre Dame University.

Putting the Pieces Together

Attention to the experience of the participants is not a new consideration in liturgical celebration. As a matter of fact, it is as old as any theological reflection about common prayer. God invites our worship not for God's benefit but for our own. Because only when we focus on God's love and care, forgiveness and grace, do we get ourselves together and find our *place*.

Attention to the experience of the participants is not new, despite the lack of it in the period of liturgical decadence from which we are now emerging. Some decades ago, in *Orate Fratres* (now *Worship*), the late Gerald Vann commented on the statement of a famous European Catholic that "the idea of conducting services primarily for the edification of the faithful smacks of Protestantism." Vann wrote: "Alas for St. Thomas. Alas for St. Paul's great guiding 'rubric' in 1 Corinthians 14:26. Alas for every theologian who has written *On Prayer*, from Origen and St. Cyprian to St. Thomas and Suarez, who has been at pains to explain that we 'address God' not to 'edify' him, but precisely to 'edify' ourselves."

A modern recovery of the gospel's personalist emphasis has enabled us again in our time to attend to the experience of the participants in worship, whether they are children or adults or both. Attention to their experience has brought us along far beyond our "vernacular-time" fascination with words and texts—to a renewed appreciation of the multi-leveled and multi-dimensioned communication of good liturgy, involving the sensual and sensible as well as the rational, the body as well as the mind, the emotions and feelings as well as the intellect.

RITES NEED RHYTHM

When experience, rather than merely instruction, is asserted again as a primary test of good common prayer, then the sustained involvement of all participants comes to be seen clearly as a requirement. Anything but sustained involvement—e.g., boredom, distraction, day-dreaming—is the enemy of good experience. Such a sustained involvement in turn requires variety, rhythm, alternation in the structure or format or progression of any service of public worship. While adults can sustain attention for longer periods and can deal with more abstract language, the principle holds for all age groups with undiminished force.

All of us need the variety and alternation we find in the traditional structures of liturgical rites. It is apparent in the hours, the eucharist, the other sacraments. In each of the traditional structures, we can discern and feel a certain rhythm: not only a beginning, a middle, and an end, but also alternation among persons and groups of persons, among groupings of elements into a preparation and a building up and a climax and a descent, between sound and silence, between movement and stillness, between song and speech, between the familiar and the spontaneous, between proclamation and reflection, between word and deed.

The difference between children's liturgies and adult liturgies is not in these various and necessary alternations, which any group of human beings requires in order to sustain involvement and participation. One difference, however, will certainly be that the elements to be alternated in children's liturgies *must be* more brief and more concrete than the various parts of a liturgy with adults. Critical requirements for children, this brevity and concreteness of each element or part of a rite are frequently advantageous for adults as well. So we need not feel that we are depriving the latter group of spiritual sustenance when we take those requirements into account in our planning.

OF PROCESSIONS AND PUNCTUATION

Some examples may help clarify what we have called "rhythm" or alternation in liturgical structures. A reading is never followed by another reading. It may be followed by reflective song, or reflective silence, or on special occasions a mime or dance reflection on it. But the proclamation of a reading has to stand out as something integral, something worth reflecting about. Responsory psalms or songs, therefore, are to be sung, not read. If they cannot be sung, they are better omitted in favor of silence.

Any processional movement, whether of ministers or of congregation as a whole, is aided by song, or at least by instrumental music. In the eucharist, this is true above all of the most important procession, the climactic procession for the sharing of holy communion. The activity of the communion procession and sharing and song, for the sake of a good rhythm or alternation, yields to what? To more song? Would it not be more appropriate to see that it yields to stillness and silence?

A service of public worship, like any other public assembly, requires punctuation and definition. Minimally, for example, the punctuation of a specific greeting by the presider at the beginning and a clear dismissal at the end is indispensable for a feeling of shape and form. Beyond that, ritual action demands and deserves the kind of orchestration or choreography that builds gradually, smoothly, steadily toward a climax, and then, rather swiftly and gently, moves to dismissal.

All of this is common sense as well as liturgical tradition and law. Unfortunately, it takes a special effort to apply common sense to habitual actions.

Ritual celebration, because of its habitual character, tends to escape the scrutiny of common sense. Planners, therefore, need to look very carefully not only at the individual elements, the various parts, of any celebration, but also at the sequence of the elements or parts, their relation to one another and to the entire action.

Vocal prayers must not be piled upon vocal prayers, nor song upon song, nor gesture upon gesture. If any of these is worth doing, it deserves definition, integrity, uncluttered articulation. Each deserves to be taken seriously enough to be permitted to stand on its own feet, to accomplish its particular purpose, and to help us move on in a progressive and coherent fashion.

NO PLACE FOR "FILLERS"

In other words, we have no "fillers" in a well-planned liturgical action. No part or element is introduced simply because we have to pass the time. We do not "throw in" a song because someone likes it, or interpose a gesture because it is familiar, or include a dance because we have a dancer. If someone likes a song, if a gesture is familiar, if local talent is available, that is certainly a plus. But anything that is to be part of a liturgy must pass the tests of quality and appropriateness.

No art form, for example, is in and of itself alien to or unacceptable in liturgical celebration. This is just as true of dance and mime and drama and film or slide projection as it is of music and painting and sculpture and stained glass. The question is not, "Which arts are acceptable?" The proper questions regard the quality of the art and its appropriate use.

"Children are open
and in the process
of formation."

Quality is no less important for children's celebrations than it is for adult or general ones. Perhaps it is even more important when dealing with children, because children are open and in the process of formation. Children still have a chance of achieving a greater appreciation of beauty, authenticity, craftsmanship, skill, color and shape, texture, etc. Most adults are profoundly affected by our culture's general insensitivity and even blindness with regard to quality.

Applied to human talents employed in celebration (e.g., readers, song leader, singers, instrumentalists, acolytes, hosts or ushers, dancers, actors, presiders), quality has reference to training, competence, skill, practice. Applied to objects employed either as part of the environment of celebration or within the celebrative action (e.g., building interior, seating, decoration, altar, candles, cross, vessels, vesture, book), quality involves craftsmanship, art, honesty and genuineness, simplicity, beauty of form and color, the personal stamp of an artist, and similar considerations. If many of us adults have been deprived of this kind of sensitivity, we owe our children an opportunity—by every means possible, including liturgical celebration—for a broader and richer development of their human faculties.

All that can be said, however, about quality environment, quality performance, quality symbols and art and visuals is not enough. Liturgy makes even greater demands than that. For liturgy, as we have indicated, is a community action with definition and orchestration. Every element, every part, must be appropriate. Appropriateness is a criterion that must be applied as rigorously as quality. With reference to art objects, we have to ask: Is it an integral and harmonious part of an environment suitable for celebration? Or is it simply clutter and irrelevance?

With reference to talents or ministries or elements we might consider for a particular service of worship, appropriateness can be judged by similar questions: Does it support and enhance the action of the rite? Or is it a kind of interruption or intermission in the normal progress of the particular liturgy? If we can answer "Yes" to the former, we can embrace and employ any art and any element. If the answer to the latter question is "Yes," then, no matter how good the quality, it cannot claim a place in liturgy.

This section was written by Robert W. Hovda, author of the Manual of Celebration *and* From Ashes to Easter: Design for Parish Renewal, *and an editor on the Liturgical Conference staff. Father Hovda is a priest of the Diocese of Fargo, North Dakota.*

Liturgy
Is More
Than Words

Music

In a recent conversation with a friend of ours who has been doing work with children's liturgies forever, it seems, she put the question right to us: "Why more 'stuff' on children's music? There's oodles around now!" She's right, of course. One can find a pre-planned package for any theme, complete with rituals, words, music, chords, and a quickie course in how to play the guitar or form a rhythm band. Search through the better religion teachers' manuals or write to the major liturgical music publishers and you'll find more material than you can deal with. But the question is, will you always find the material that you want to deal with?

A great portion of the material published today is aimed at the informal setting. It envisions a very loosely structured environment in which the young people are encouraged to be spontaneous and open. This, of course, is extremely healthy, particularly when we consider the staid and rather rigorous environment that most of us were raised in. (Truth to tell, the parents and other adult leaders often find these celebrations as freeing and fun as the children do—maybe even more so.) But we must also see that this kind of liturgy—especially if it represents the total liturgical experience of children—can have liabilities too.

The informal liturgy which has the children gathered around the old oak tree in the church yard, tying yellow ribbons to its lower branches and singing, "Tie a Yellow Ribbon," has merit as a kind of reconciliation rite. But it also lacks something. It lacks a connecting link to the church's ritual history. It is a rite apart. If the child is exposed only to this kind of music and liturgical celebration, how will (s)he be integrated into the broader context of the liturgical life of the church? Liturgical music for children must address itself to where the children *are*, yes . . . but we are also called to lead them forward to new depths of meaning. This is what true richness is. Part of the growth of a child into adolescence includes a gradual exposure to those things which are a bit above or beyond what (s)he can respond to immediately. Let me give an example.

I [Ed] once led a youth choir composed of young people aged 11 to about 16. It was a folk choir and what we did we did well—after much hard work on their part. But a couple of times a year, at Easter and Christmas, we would do some work with the parish adult choir. Our most outstanding experience with them was working on Randall Thompson's *Alleluia* for Easter. It is an

extremely difficult piece to sing well and the director would have it no other
way. The kids kicked and screamed all the way through it, but they were
faithful to rehearsals. When finally this vast, random collection of notes became one beautiful musical expression in their minds, they fell in love with
it. It was sung in the car going to picnics right along with "He Ain't Heavy"
and all the others. Their ears were opened to new musical possibilities. Most
importantly, they discovered a new and deeper significance for Easter and
what an "Alleluia" it is.

It seems most appropriate that on the occasion of major feasts we strive very
hard to develop an enthusiasm for the more formal kinds of musical experiences in worship. During these times the church is at its best, retelling the
basic mysteries of salvation for *all* to hear. (One caution: Because much of
what we are going to say from here on deals with this more formal setting,
it is good to remember that these events are not intended to replace the less
structured and spontaneous but, together with them, provide for the earlier
mentioned rich liturgical music life for young people.)

SOME PRINCIPLES AND SUGGESTIONS

Because of the nature of the "high" feasts themselves, the music for them must be special—specially selected, specially prepared, and specially integrated into the entire celebration. Here, we will combine some principles with some practical suggestions which can be helpful under a variety of local circumstances. We're presupposing that you're the generous soul who said "yes" to the liturgy committee chairperson; that you would take on the job of involving the children in the music aspect of the major feasts of the church year. There are a number of ways you can go about your task. You can just fill in the liturgical blanks, so to speak, or you can make an effort to apply some principles to your efforts. In the end, it's not so important that you use *these* principles as it is that you use *some* set of guiding principles.

1. *Music is not a bauble!* We do not have music in a celebration because it's always been there. It is not an adornment. It is an integral part of the celebration just as speech, color and light, movement and silence are. It is a mode of expression which allows the worshiping group to share with feeling and conviction what they believe. Throughout the whole of human history, believers have chosen music as the way to say best what their experience of God and his deeds has been for them. When developing celebrations around the feasts of, say, Christmas and Easter—celebrations in which children will be involved—one temptation is to go to your song collection and reach in for the appropriate ornaments. That is not bad, but *where* and *how* you place them on the tree is a critical point. You must first determine, with the help of the other persons responsible for the overall planning, what this particular celebration is attempting to communicate. Each of the great feasts is so rich that it is almost meaningless to say, "We're trying to communicate Christmas." As you go to your collection of music you must go with a direction in mind. The music might alter your direction slightly, shed new light on it, but it must be selected with the idea of contributing to something larger than itself. In other words, there may be some Christmas celebrations where "Silent Night" or "The Little Drummer Boy" just won't fit. You may realize that these particular songs are better suited to a time prior to the celebration itself. If this concentration on selection and placement is not done, the ebb and flow of the celebration simply cannot be established. (A way to tell whether or not you have succeeded in this regard is whether people comment about the celebration as a whole or whether they comment only about the music. If your selections are integrated into the larger celebration, you cannot help but establish a total effect.

2. *The high feasts deserve special music.* How do children find out that something is special? They find out that *they* are special because of the way their parents react to them. They celebrate their birthdays, take them to interesting places, listen to their problems and experiences. Children know that guests are special because a special meal is prepared, or because the good dishes come out, or they eat in the dining room, with linen. Wine is served, or flowers are placed on the table. Without these kinds of signs there would be no such thing as "special."

The same kinds of criteria can be used in selecting music for the special feasts. Special preparations are made and the children should be included even in this stage of the process. The special feast, unlike the more spontaneous celebration (which can also take up much preparation time), must include the children's active participation in the preparation. With music, this is a good time to introduce harmony or singing in rounds. It might also be time to bring in someone special to teach the singing (more on that a little later). Perhaps particular attention might be given to the background of some of the music. Special parts can be given out for solo and small group presentation—by children as well as adults.

It's often said with vacations that half the fun is getting there. The same can be said of music at the great feasts—half the meaning is in the efforts made to make the event truly special.

3. *Special music takes special preparation.* If you are that person who willingly accepted this task of involving the children in the music for the major feasts, we would suggest that you first choose a team of adults to work with you. On this team, as we hinted at earlier, should be someone who is trained in music and can handle this end of the task. Have an initial meeting where you discuss the theme and format of the celebration and place tasks into competent hands. Stay in touch throughout the planning and preparation time to be sure that the "parts" are not wandering away from the "whole." The point here is quite simple: teaching songs is quite different from teaching a group to sing or teaching them music. There is much more to it than memorizing words and a reasonable facsimile of the melody. Many of our contemporary Christian churches have become very derelict in their duty to teach people how to sing (e.g., often sloppiness is accepted in favor of volume). We lose sight of the fact that a song is a complete unit, a blending of words and music to achieve meaning and not just words set to a melody. Competent people have the skills to achieve the blend. They also have the background to insure that aesthetics are adhered to. There is great advantage in having such a person "on call" for these special times. If such a person is not in your congregation, we suggest calling the local elementary or junior high school to see if, perhaps, there might not be someone there who would be willing to assume such a task. It might be necessary to pay for such services but the long and short range benefits can be tremendous.

4. *Traditional music is not the only kind of "good" music.* Once we begin talking about music as "good" we must presuppose that there must be some that is "bad." It is, however, totally wrong to equate "good" with traditional and "bad" with contemporary. It is likewise wrong to confuse "good" with appropriate. Some very good music can be very inappropriate—as far as the theme is concerned, or as far as the children are concerned. It might be inappropriate because it is too difficult to sing properly or because the lyrics are too symbolic or sophisticated. The tendency at these major celebrations is to go immediately to the more traditional material. This can be a mistake—much is available that is good, appropriate, and contemporary. Some "folk" tunes are also good and appropriate. A rich mixture of many of these

sources, thoughtfully blended into one celebration, is usually successful. Again, we cannot stress enough that if a professional person can be secured for this task, many of your problems can be lessened.

DOCTORING TUNES TO ENHANCE CELEBRATION

Before pursuing this topic any further, let us hasten to say that if you are going to arrange or adapt songs that have a copyright you must seek permission from the publisher. This is a very practical reason for beginning your planning early. Generally, we have found this relatively easy to do and publishers are quite cooperative.

In the section which follows we will share with you some of the experiences and ideas we have had and have heard of—not in an effort to tempt you to do the same, but more as "idea starters." We will simply take some simple musical ideas and illustrate briefly what can be done.

ADVENT AND CHRISTMAS

"O Come, O Come, Emmanuel." There are a number of themes in this hymn: promise, exile, the power of God, etc. The one we chose to work on was "longing." It seemed to us that the music, especially, contributed to this theme when it was sung slowly and deliberately. To emphasize this theme we divided the group into three sections. Each section kept repeating the first four words of the song, in a sort of round, to get the effect of pleading. Each section would hold the last "come" until the next section had finished its part. This was done in the dark to add to the effect—the contrast of children's voices developing this kind of mood is quite striking. When each section had done its part twice, the entire group sang the rest of the verse, ending before the "Rejoice, Rejoice." The other verses served as the musical responsorial for an entire worship service, interspersed with readings, tableau, and a slide presentation. Toward the end of one such service we had a solo presentation, by one of the older girls, of a contemporary interpretation of the "Magnificat" found in Volume One of the *Young Christian Hymnal*. (Incidentally, we weren't too crazy about the refrain in this, so we left it out.)

"Wayfarin' Stranger." This is an old American folk tune which has a number of arrangements and versions, most of which suited our purposes. We used

it to highlight the character of Abraham as the father of the promise, changing the verses slightly to suit his role. (This is something that can be readily done with "real" folk music because it is generally public domain. However, it is not considered aesthetically good to change the entire lyric, as many have done, since this violates the song's roots.) Other folk songs were used to expand on other great Old Testament figures leading up to the birth of Jesus.

"Virgin Mary." This is another traditional folk tune. Its beauty lies in its simplicity—Virgin Mary had a little baby, o yeh! Glory Halleluia! It starts out softly with only snapping fingers for accompaniment. Wood blocks could be used just as well. Eventually, guitar accompaniment enters. We used it as one of a number of selections before the Christmas midnight mass which dealt with the theme of Christmas without neon.

LENT AND EASTER

"Were You There?" This spiritual can be used very effectively with young and old voices combined, because it has such a wide vocal range. The adults can begin the song, by putting the question to the children. There is a brief pause and the children pick up the question, putting it to the adults. The rest of the song can likewise be divided up according to vocal range. A slide presentation can be woven into the song on the theme of our brotherhood in Jesus. It can be very effective at a family penitential celebration. There is a caution here: This song is very graphic. If slides are to be used in connection with it, every effort should be made not to suggest the interpretation that every little peccadillo is like "nailin' in the nails." A broader approach should be used, more in the direction of our call to heal pain and reconcile our differences in the family.

"The King of Glory." This song can also be found in Volume One of the Young Christian Hymnal. It is especially appropriate for Palm Sunday. Harmony can easily be taught for the chorus; a variety of interesting things can be done with the verses. Actually, if you look closely at the verses you can almost envision the Palm Sunday scenario: Jesus entering town, excitement building, people asking questions, others responding according to what they have heard and seen. You can turn your congregation of young people into a crowd with all singing the chorus and small groups singing the various verses. The first verse, which is a question and a response, can be handled by two good soloists. It makes for an exciting and effective entrance procession.

"I Thank You God!" Easter is the feast of Christians, and hence defies the notion of any kind of separate liturgy for children. However, once again, it is essential that the younger members of the community have an opportunity to participate in the event meaningfully. Using the theme of "new life" for the entire celebration, we tried the following at the gift procession. "I Thank You God" (lyrics by e.e. cummings, music by Lloyd Pfautsch, Lawson-Gould Music Publishers, Inc., L.G. 51215) is a beautiful, light and simple song, "mis-phrased" as only Cummings can. Its celebrative words and music are highly imagistic and can be a beautiful backdrop for a gift procession of "spring things." The entire congregation can sing the first four words with the briefest rehearsal—in fact, if a cantor intones it, they need only respond. The children's voices pick up the middle lyrics and an adult choir can finish the last line, in its four parts, at the end of the processional.

It would probably be in order to say something about the other great Christian feasts, but that is not the purpose of this particular section. We have simply tried to capture for you some of our feelings about the involvement of children, at various levels and in a variety of ways, in the celebration of these especially sublime moments in Christian living. We hope that sharing our experiences will provide you with some direction and stimulate your own thinking about new possibilities.

The peace of the Lord go with us all in this most challenging ministry.

This section was written by Ed and Diane Murray of Richmond, Virginia. Ed holds a degree in religious education from The Catholic University of America, served three years as a parish director of religious education, and is presently diocesan Director of Religious Education and Liturgy in Richmond. Diane's interests are in early childhood religious education and liturgy, with special emphasis on family religious development. She is presently teaching religion in two Catholic high schools in Richmond.

Mime, Improvisation and Drama

"Movement is the one characteristic by which life is most readily recognized," Sanford Jones wrote in *Children's Liturgies*. In a very useful essay (to which the reader of these words will want to turn before (s)he continues here), Jones points out that for growing children, there are two developmental phases of movement: (1) movement as a sign of control, and (2) movement as expression. Competence in the movements associated with the control of their own bodies and limbs must invariably precede any competence in the movements associated with the expression and communication of meanings.

Mime, improvisation, dance and drama all represent forms of expressive movement. In their most sophisticated expression, each of these forms has developed into a separate discipline of extraordinary subtlety, precision, and richness; think of the work of Marcel Marceau or the Royal Shakespeare Company at Stratford. Professional competence in mime and drama continues to enrich our lives perhaps even more universally now through the medium of television.

But in their most elemental and primitive expression, mime and drama are part of the play of every growing child. It is almost a universal human pleasure to take delight in pretending, in dressing up, or in acting out our myths and fantasies (and often too our fears). From so-called "body-language," to the stylized gestures of ritual, to the "let's pretend" games of childhood, to the inspired discipline of an Alvin Ailey or a Laurence Olivier, mime and movement are simply part of our human experience, in which all of us take part. We are all of us performers, actors, or dancers at some point or other in our human experience; it only remains to remind ourselves of that from time to time, and to devote some energy to trying to understand this universal "language" to improve our own competence in it. And of course, to devote some energy to training our children in it, as well.

HOW DO BODIES SPEAK?

A useful exercise for anyone eager to learn more about expressive movement would be a simple ongoing study of so-called body language. The body and the way it moves represents perhaps the most elemental instrument for human communication. What does it "say" in this or that social encounter? How does it "speak"? To ask these questions is to begin to teach ourselves some of the basic "vocabulary" of drama and mime. And you can do it anywhere, unnoticed and unembarrassed! It's great fun. So for example:

You're at the beach. Some few feet away, a handsome young man reclines on his towel, leaning on one elbow, looking out toward the water. He is bronzed by the sun; his teeth are straight and glistening white. Now a lovely young woman approaches along the beach. She notices the young man almost with a start. She inhales deeply and her stomach muscles do not relax after the breath, but rein in her belly; her right hand raises to her head and her fingers comb through her hair; as she walks by, her chin lifts and she arches her head back on her slender neck ever so slightly. (The plot has already begun to thicken!)

To an alert observer, there is a wonderful richness of meaning in this little exchange. The young woman has quite likely been impressed at the sight of the young man. Immediately, perhaps unconsciously, she begins to utilize a whole vocabulary of "preening" gestures: the tightening of the stomach, the arranging of the hair, the arching of the neck. (As for the young man, he has quite likely been "preening" as well!)

Or consider this situation: You are on a busy street corner, waiting for a bus. Across the street stand three men in apparently earnest conversation. You cannot hear the words, but their gesture and posture tell you much: two of the men stand side by side, taking positions across from the third, and at a distinct angle to him. They stand with feet slightly apart, weight evenly balanced, their arms crossed at their chests. It would not be necessary to know that they are both frowning, but you note with a glance that they are. As for the third man, he is moving his arms in agitation, and shifting his weight from foot to foot.

An argument, perhaps? Surely at least some significant difference of opinion or viewpoint. And the speaker seems to be outnumbered. Students of such things tell us that as much as 55% of everything you learn about me you learn non-verbally; that is, from my posture and gesture and facial expression, my clothing, my walk and movements—my body language. Another 38% is still not purely "verbal" but rather vocal: the tone of my voice, the speed and volume with which I speak, the pitch and modulation of my words, etc. Finally, a slim 7% is verbal: the actual cognitive content of what I say. Those statistics ought to give nightmares to a preacher . . . or a teacher. But it's no news at all to an actor.

FROM IMPROVISATION TO PROFESSIONALISM

How may drama, mime, and movement be utilized in the Christian formation of our children? Let me suggest three levels of production, ranging from the simplest to the most complex.

1. The first type of mime or drama is the simplest and most elemental, and in many ways the most immediate and satisfying. It's the type of artless play-acting that could be improvised, on the spot in, say, a class in Sunday school or religious education, where the motive is simply to impress some of the meanings of a story more deeply into the children's consciousness, and to give them an opportunity to express a response. Or the motive might be actually therapeutic—a kind of dramatic role-play that's done only for the sake of the participants themselves. Considerations of setting, costume, props, or make-up are minimal, if not actually non-existent. Such brief, simple dramatizations can serve their own purposes, in their own right, quite adequately and even charmingly, as self-expression, or pedagogy, with no other reason for being than that they are fun to do, children love them, and they learn by them. But they can also serve as sketches or idea-starters for more full-blown productions.

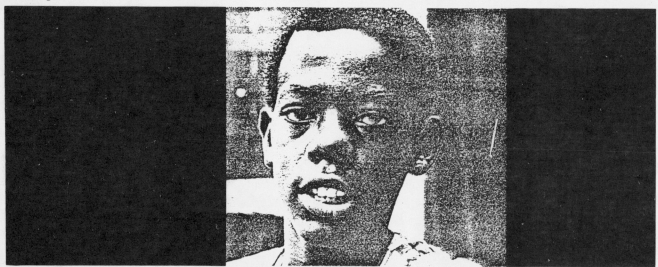

2. The second level of production is somewhat more rehearsed and disciplined. This is the type of drama that might be utilized in a larger or more formal setting: a celebration or service of worship in church, presented before an audience of others than one's peers—the familiar Christmas pageant

comes to mind. If the first level of production could be compared to a group of singers gathered around a piano for a spontaneous hymn-sing, this second level might be analagous to a choir anthem on Sunday morning. It is more professional, more disciplined, and our motive is not simply to express ourselves, but also to communicate that expression to others.

3. The third level of production would be the most professional of all: perhaps a full-blown drama presented for a community audience, with publicity beforehand—and perhaps even critical reviews after! Presumably adults or young people would assume important roles here.

Before we turn to a simple example of each, let me say a word about those terms "professional" and "amateur," and about "spectator" and "participant" as well. In the sense used above, the first level of production could perhaps be described as the most "amateur," the third the most "professional." But the word "amateur" at its root means simply "one who loves" to do what he's doing. And liturgy is preeminently the work of amateur. It would be a terrible distortion to insist that there is no place for the "amateur" spirit, or even the "amateur" competence—even at level three above. There is less place for sloppiness or shodiness, certainly. But any human art in the service of the gospel will always be gloriously amateur, at its best. And that is good news, not bad. We do what we do because we love to do it.

The same goes for those polarities "spectator" and "participant." Kierkegaard has pointed out how liturgy demands participants—actors in the drama—not mere spectators, dispassionately observing, but all of us together deeply involved in the doing. Level one above presumes that all, or nearly all of those present are involved. Does level three presume less? There is a sense of course in which we cannot invite the public to attend our play (as in level three) and then *demand* of everyone there that they somehow participate. Yet this must always remain our goal—without coercion, so to construct the dynamics of the drama as to invite each spectator to become as fully a participant as (s)he is capable of becoming. Even TV commercials attempt as much. The Christian life demands not only loving amateurs, but also active participants. We ought to keep that principle in mind.

LET'S ACT IT OUT!

As for examples: Here's a level-one production: We're in a church-school class with eight children and a teacher. We've read the story of the good Samaritan and the teacher suggests we act it out. The children respond (let's hope) with enthusiasm. The teacher has prepared beforehand, and invites volunteers: Who will play the man journeying from Jerusalem to Jericho? Johnny raises his hand; from the closet of "dress up" clothes, the teacher gives him a battered felt hat to wear on his head, and a briefcase to carry, with $100 in play money inside. The volunteers for the "robbers" are equipped with red bandannas to tie around the face like Jesse James; the "Samaritan" is also given a bandanna to wear around his neck. (He *looks* like an outsider, with his bandanna; almost like a robber! But he acts differently.) He's also given a couple of band-aids for his first aid. The "priest" is given a biretta to wear; the "levite" an academic mortarboard. The "innkeeper" carries a linen towel folded over his arm, like a waiter (his "maniple"?); there might even be a "donkey": a (stronger) child on hands and knees, with a square of folded blanket over his back as saddle. There, in that corner, beside the bookcase, is "Jerusalem"; there, by the fireplace, is "Jericho"; the "robbers" hide behind these chairs. (The children of course participate in these decisions.) And the "robbers" will remember, won't they, to just *pretend* to hit? All right, let's act it out!

At level two, such a simple pantomime might also serve, embellished with two or three congregational hymns. (And without the human "donkey," of course, since that might provoke snickers, apart from the simpler context of a group of peers.) A little more elaboration in costuming might be in order at level two; certainly some disciplined rehearsal time. (Four to six rehearsals should be enough for a 15-minute presentation.) Will the children memorize their lines, or will there be a narrator? A narrator affords the simplest solution: such a brief dramatization could accompany, for example, the reading of the gospel account by a lector in the context of the actual liturgy. Or it could follow the liturgical reading, in lieu of homily. Or it could be presented as a kind of offertory anthem.

A level-three production of the same material would require, needless to say, even more elaboration: more time in rehearsals, more attention to expression-for-the-sake-of-communication. Perhaps we'll have a brass quintet; perhaps a lighting gallery, with colored floodlights and movable spots (these can both be improvised with tin cans and light bulbs). A backstage crew might be in order, to set the stage and handle props. Maybe we could use a real donkey! Do we need printed publicity? A printed playbill to identify the actors, singers, dancers, stagehands? To tell something about the play itself? Will we use a master of ceremonies to introduce the hymns to be sung, or to lead the singing? These are the kinds of considerations that you'd expect to deal with on level three.

THE ELEMENTS OF DRAMA

But at all three levels we will need to know something about the elements of drama. Your own constant observation of the way people move and interact will provide the best training. But here's a checklist of some that count:

1. *Preeminently, position, posture, and movement.* These are the three elements above all others that help to express and communicate meanings in mime and drama. Position in the space is foremost: consider the relative positions of the three men on the street corner in the example above. Strength or dominance can be suggested by closeness to the audience or height above other actors; all eyes will turn to the person who is standing in a group of people seated; to the solitary figure standing stage left apart

from a massed group stage right. What postures suggest stability and assurance? How can I move in such a way as to communicate nervousness and apprehension? To ask—and answer!—such questions is to move closer to your goal.

There is a tremendously rich and subtle "vocabulary" of position, posture and movement to be discovered—and to be invented!—by anyone who takes the time. (Another worthwhile exercise: turn on the TV, but turn off the sound. See if you can interpret meanings with the visual "vocabulary" alone.)

2. *Voice and speech*. Again, don't forget to make use of all the rich vocal possibilities: speed, pitch, volume, repetition, inflection, overlapping, rhythm, modulation. (Our children, ages 9 and 11, recently attended with us a splendid Stratford production of Shakespeare's *Love's Labor's Lost*, and comprehended an incredible proportion of what went on; chiefly, I suppose, through posture, gesture, and vocal nuances, and in spite of the literal meanings of the words Shakespeare used.)

3. *Setting*. Movement takes place always within some environmental setting. Simply to clear a space—to unclutter it by removing everything you don't need—is to "set the stage," and to set it adequately, for most church drama. I've seen productions of *Noah's Flood*, for example, that did *not* need in the least the elaborate superstructures of wood and canvas that were used to construct an "ark" onstage; the imagination was actually crippled. (Far better, I felt, to have said, the altar is our "ark" tonight; let's pretend this processional cross is the mast; and so on.)

4. *Costume*. The great Olaf Hartman maintains that church drama should never concern itself with "period" biblical costumes, but utilize instead (a) street clothes or (b) vestments or (c) dancers' tights and leotards or some combination of these. I agree. Attempts to suggest biblical or even medieval costume by the use of Uncle Henry's castoff bathrobe, for example, are doomed to failure; they're only laughable. For a Christmas drama, why not real richly-tailored copes for the Three Kings and for Herod? Cassock and cotta for Mary and Joseph? Tights and hooded sweatshirts for the Shepherds?

5. *Make-up*. At all three levels of production, I'd be as wary of inauthenticity in make-up as in costume. No beards, please, unless it's the actor's own. (Why *not* a beardless Jesus, for example?) I'd make it a point to allow actors and mimes to wear wristwatch, ring or eye glasses: it helps the audience to contemporize the action. But discreet make-up, like discreet costuming, can enrich a production at level three, if it's done by a real master.

6. *Lighting*. Drama can surely be enhanced too by effective lighting, especially at level three, but also at level-two productions. Remember too: Pools of light can define space and establish mood as well as illuminate action. Experiment with the possibilities in your setting before investing in equipment.

7. *Music*. Parish musicians should be enlisted for their contribution as soon

as you begin to consider anything more elaborate than a simple level-one production. I'd suggest utilizing the congregation or audience itself as well: incorporate the singing of congregational hymns or psalms or chants as part of the action. It helps the spectator become a participant.

SENSITIVITY TO "SHAPE"

One word about "shape" before we turn to a producer's time-line. An alert director or producer will be sensitive to three realities:

A. *Sensitive to the "shape" of the drama itself.* I take it as one of the contributions of the Judaeo-Christian understanding of history that most of us in the West can hardly imagine a play or drama without a specific "shape." It's the responsibility of the director to discover in his drama at least four developmental stages:

1. Setting the scene, and filling in necessary background and characterizations. ("I am Satan and I'm going to test this Woman and this Man to see how faithful they will be . . . ")

2. The plot thickens. (Eve and Satan engage in dialog; his arguments begin to convince . . .)

3. The story reaches a climax, sometimes with a secondary climax as well. (Eve takes the apple; she goes to Adam and he eats; they hear the voice of God: "Adam, where are you? . . . ")

4. The resolution or *dénouement*: the issues are resolved in a way that satisfies the viewer/hearer. (God enacts his judgment but also promises his rescue; Adam and Eve leave the Garden . . .)

B. *Sensitive to the "shape" of individual scenes within the larger drama.* Frequently a single actor will be called upon to modify the mood or pace of the play within a few lines or even words of dialog. Be sensitive to the hinges, the turning points, of individual scenes.

C. *Sensitive to the "shape" of individual actions or speeches.* In most instances, nouns and verbs carry the weight of meaning in the English language. (Who is it—airline stewardesses?—who have taught us to accent prepositions in speech?) Remind your actors: nouns and verbs. All is nouns and verbs.

PRODUCER'S TIME-LINE

Finally, here's a kind of producer's time-line. If you're interested in putting together a level-two or three type of production, you should be giving attention to the following:

1. *Note the production level.* You'll want to demand a higher level of competence in level-three production than in level one. The audience will have more fully developed expectations.

2. *Choosing a play.* There's a great deal of material available. For the simplest mime and dramatization, Bible stories from, for instance, the *Arch* series of children's books are great, or the *Little People's Paperbacks.* More ambitious productions (level two and three) will want to look into some of the great literature, such as medieval mystery plays.

3. *Casting.* Physical appearance is important in casting, of course, but even more crucial is the quality known as "presence." For important roles, try to choose only those persons who have that magnetic ability to command attention, even when they're in repose.

4. *Determine the setting.* Once again, imagination in director and in audience should not be underestimated. The simplest of settings can be very effective. (For our *Noah,* we chose a city park, with a real boat as part of the existing play equipment; it was a setting that cried out to be used!)

5. *Block the action.* The director will have to spend some time alone with his script and a half a dozen chessmen, perhaps, moving them around as the action of the play dictates. ("Now King Belshazzar moves from his throne over here by the candlestick, and Daniel makes his speech moving here."—that kind of thing. Chessmen or clothespins help.)

6. *Rehearse with the cast.* After you yourself have blocked the action, then move your actors through the action, ignoring niceties of speech for the time being, and concentrating only on the actors' movements. *Transitions* in action, as in speech, are once again very tricky. Your first concern at this stage of rehearsal should be only to make clear where each actor enters, where (s)he stands and moves, and so on. Gross gestures first. Gross movements. Then begin to refine.

7. *Line rehearsals.* As your actors become more confident with their movements, begin to devote attention to their speech, and how their voices "project." Perhaps several line rehearsals will help: just words, forgetting action (you can all be sitting around a table for this). Concentrate this time on meaning, inflection, rhythm. And on nouns and verbs. Make sure all actors pick up cues quickly.

8. *Establish pace.* Some parts of the drama will want to proceed at a leisurely tempo; at other points, you'll want to race along. Check the "shape" of the action or the scene to give you clues. Nothing is worse than drama that drags.

9. *Determine mood and style.* You'll be answering these questions as you go along. How "real" or how "ritual" might you want this to appear? Considerations of color, costuming, and lighting make a big difference in mood.

(Do you want your play to have an earthy, brown-and-grey mood? Is the mood light and sunny, yellow-and-orange-and-pink?)

One final exhortation: Don't be intimidated by the smooth professionalism you see in TV or movies or theater. Anyone with zest for life—and imagination!—can put together a charming church drama, at least on level one, that's greatly satisfying to all. And level three requires only a little more experience.

This section was written by Paul F. Bosch, Lutheran Campus Pastor at Syracuse University, author of A Worship Workbench, *as well as many magazine articles and filmstrips, and past president of the Lutheran Society for Worship, Music and the Arts.*

A Time for Dancing

Of all the elements that comprise a liturgical celebration—whether it be for adults, or children, or groups of adults and children—gesture and movement have been given the least amount of attention. Persons planning liturgies continue to feel secure in the realm of words and ill-at-ease with other art forms involving the body. A common misconception is that the integration of body movement, gesture, etc. in a celebration is possible only with the help of a professional dancer; if the services of such an artist are not available in the parish, that is taken as indication enough that work in this area must be postponed until a later day.

What follows are some simple suggestions under the headings of Blessings, Chants, and Dance—just enough, perhaps, to give confidence to beginners: confidence not only to make use of what is provided, but to begin to create their own patterns of movement, to share them with children, and to invite the children to use their own powers of creativity.

BLESSINGS

The Lord bless you and keep you!
The Lord let his face shine upon you,
   and be gracious to you!
The Lord look upon you kindly
   and give you peace!
Numbers 6:24-26

Blessings originate from God and are a communication of life. When we bless we do so in reference to our wish or prayer that God will bless someone and give him the abundance of life. Usually a blessing is given by a person who is a true leader, i.e. a priest, the father or mother in a family, etc. When creatures bless God, the blessing is in the form of a prayer of thanks.

In the recent past we have seen a re-embracing of the ancient forms of blessings. In the new sacramentary we see re-instituted the rite of Blessing and Sprinkling of Holy Water. With sensitivity for very young children, the Directory for Masses with Children suggests that these members could be made to feel part of the celebration if they were "brought in at the end of Mass to be blessed together with the rest of the community."

These developments, as well as the traditions of the church, should encourage us to be creative in our use of blessings. The following experiences incorporating movement and gesture may provide a launching pad for new creative forms.

Rite of Blessing and Sprinkling of Holy Water

Note: Children are divided into four groups and placed in semi-circular fashion around the altar. Celebrant reads the following prayer as children express the prayer through movement.

ALL: Father in heaven,
Bless you for your goodness.

All movement is done slowly and deliberately.

I: Bless you for water that refreshes as it rains down on the earth after it has been warmed by the sun.

downward movement of arms in a circle in front of body

IV: Bless you for water that rushes over rocks and down mountainsides; as it cleanses us of the impurities of our own deeds.

flowing movement as though water

II: Bless you, Father, for water, that quenches our thirst; that makes us ready to speak your word fresh each day.

upward movement beginning at chin

III: Bless you for water, that gives new life to the hidden seed, to the giant oak, and to the rivers of our earth.

bowing movement from waist

ALL: Father in heaven,
Bless you for your goodness.

rising movement from waist

CELEBRANT: God you are the Father of the Great Sea. Let your
waters flow on us and be a healing for us. Give us
the new life which is your life.
(*Celebrant blesses all present with holy water.*)

In Praise of the Morning Sun—A Blessing

A story is told in New Mexico of an ancient Indian custom. The mother of
the family tells the children that in the evening the sun goes down beneath
the earth to gather all the blessings for the following day. The next day the
children greet the morning sun and ask for its blessings in a prayer of praise.
The following prayer, based on this story, might be used in a family setting
for morning praise.

From the setting of the sun
to its early rising we praise
you, God our Father.

*All movement is
done by the entire
family. Facing west
with palms down*

Each morning the light of
your sun wakes me.

*turn toward the
morning sun, rub
eyes as though
waking up*

The warmth of your sun
makes the earth fresh
with new growth.

*rising from a deep
bow*

Give us your blessings today and
continue to shine your
face on us.

*downward movement
in front of body*

Praise to God our Father
for he has been at work
even while we slept.

*flowing movement
from side to side*

Ash Wednesday Blessing in the Home

After a short discussion about what the family will do during Lent, the
eldest member of the family blesses each individual with the following prayer
while placing his hands on each person's shoulder.

God bless you with his life and the
joy of his breath within you. Help
you to live as his son/daughter; speak
as his son/daughter; act with courage.

May you be an example to our family
during this springtime in the church.

CHANTS

Chants are primitive musical art forms of expression. Chants have few varia-
tions of sound. They may be sung or spoken. Children begin chanting almost
as soon as they begin to talk. Their chants are spontaneous and are usually
accompanied by movement, e.g., jump rope chants. Often chants of children
have no real meaning in themselves but the rhythm and sound of the words
make them intriguing.

The church has used chants for centuries. These were simple melodies as in
the Gregorian chants. No adult today will ever forget the repetitive *Ora pro
nobis* of the Holy Thursday litany. Chants may relate the hopes, joys, fears,
or events of a people. They may encourage children to develop their own
simple songs of praise through these rhythmic pattern sequences.

A Spring Chant

Give thanks to God
for the earth,
And for all its beauty.

*head bent in a
praying position*

Praise him for flowers
in bloom.
And for songs of birds
give praise.

*upward movement
of arms in front of
body*

Praise God for the
morning sun,
that gives warmth
to all the earth.

Praise God for the
gentle rains,
that nourish the
planted seeds.

*downward movement
in front of body*

Praise God for the
giant oak,
as it shades the
noonday fields.

*flowing movement
above body (add own
prayer and movement
to accompany it)*

May be sung with percussion

Note: the refrain and verse may be sung at the same time, making this song a two-part round. Children can be divided into two groups, with one group singing verse one while the other sings the refrain. On verse two, the groups reverse parts, etc.

Music © 1974 Tom Parker
Words: Elizabeth Blandford

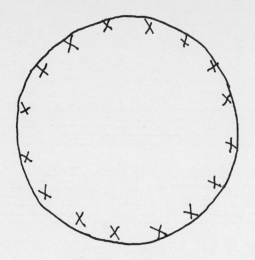

PEACE CHANT

Peace to my brother
And justice to all. (repeat twice)

Hatred and war and
cries of fear must
make room for . . .

Peace to my brother
And justice to all. (repeat twice)

Movement Patterns. All patterns should be done at least twice before chant begins to establish the rhythm. The chant and the movement are done in 4/4 time.

Pattern I: Hands on knees, right hand to left knee of next person and left hand on own right knee. Hands on own knees; left hand to right knee of next person, right hand on own left knee.

This pattern establishes the rhythm and suggests that we need others to help establish a world of peaceful people.

Pattern II: Hands on knees. Hands pushing outward in front of body. Hands on knees. Hands to side touching knees of person on either side.

This pattern suggests a pushing away from oneself all those things that are at odds with peace.

Pattern III: Hands at temples, extend or stretch arms upward. Hands on temples, hit the floor with hands. Repeat, ending with arms extended upward.

Improvise or make up new patterns; children should learn each new pattern thoroughly before progressing to the next.

PEACE CHANT

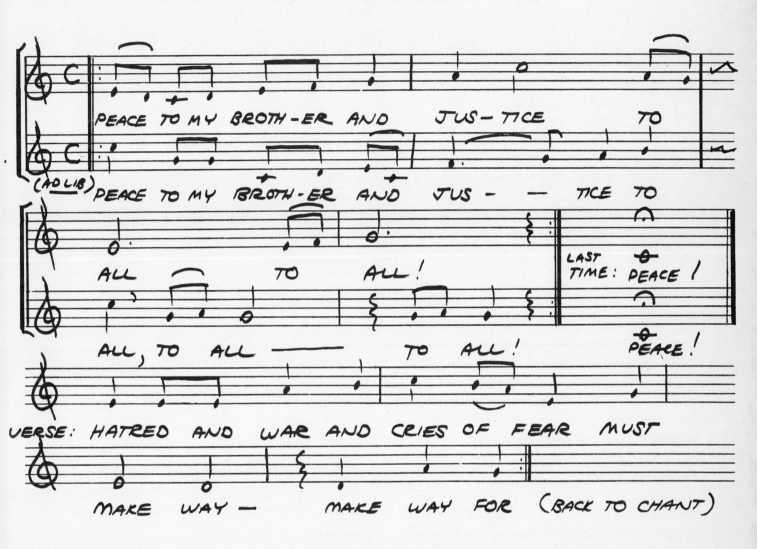

May be sung unaccompanied or with percussion.
Second part may be omitted, or added after children are familiar with first part.

Music © 1974 Tom Parker
Words: Elizabeth Blandford

This section (© 1974 by Elizabeth Blandford, SCN) was written by Elizabeth Blandford, SCN, who has given numerous workshops on liturgy, movement and gesture throughout the country. Sister is presently working in a religious education program in four parishes in the Archdiocese of Louisville, Kentucky, and is the co-author of two books on liturgy for small children, Come Out *and* Even A Worm *(World Library Publications). Her stations of the cross for children was also published by World.*

DANCE

O Come, O Come, Emmanuel

A processional dance with wreath, to be done each week of Advent. All who want to try this will line up in pairs at the back of the church. One person is the leader, and stands at the head of the double line. He or she will hold the advent wreath (which contains four unlit candles) at shoulder height, arms outstretched.

O Come, O Come, Emmanuel, and ransom captive Israel. On the words "O Come, O Come . . . " the procession moves down the aisle, arms stretched in front, palms face upward. (Practice holding the arms out in such a way as to really feel them as an extension of the self seeking God.)

That mourns in lowly exile here. Leader with the wreath stops, and all the rest bow from the waist, lowering arms. (At this point in the third verse the sequence is changed. See later directions.)

Until the son of God appear. All raise their bodies and lift up arms as before.

(Chorus) *Rejoice! Rejoice! Emmanuel.* The double line separates by everyone turning to face his partner and at the same time taking a big step backward, opening their arms wide to the sides in a joyful manner. A pathway is thus formed down which the leader dances with the wreath. (It is easy to improvise with a wreath in one's hands. Show it off, turning from side to side in a spirit of delight.) The leader must place himself at the head of the line again, in time for the next words.

Shall come to thee, O Israel. The leader continues in front dancing, as the rest link right elbows with their partners, holding their free arms raised, and swing around one time in the center of the aisle. They end with their arms down by their sides, in original lines.

Repeat the entire sequence described so far, progressing toward the altar, while all in the pews sing the second verse and chorus. By the third verse the leader places the wreath on the altar and the double line separates to the left and right and encircles the altar (leaving out the bowing). By the time of the third chorus, all are standing still facing the altar.

(Chorus—third time) *Rejoice! Rejoice! Emmanuel.* On *Rejoice, rejoice,* all take a step in toward the altar, hands held, arms lifting up. On *Emmanuel* all back away, lowering arms, dropping hands, and then lifting arms back out to the side.

Shall Come to thee, O Israel. All turn once in place, arms lifted.

Pause. The priest lights the first candle (on second week he lights the second candle, etc.) and says a prayer for Advent. He then joins the group and they

100

all circle around the altar, hands joined, as the next verse is sung, or simply hummed. The chorus movements are repeated as before (stepping toward the altar, arms raised, etc.) and all then slowly file off to their places in the church, as a final verse and chorus is sung. The wreath is left on the altar, or placed in a special spot.

Repeat this processional dance each week, teaching more and more people the dance. I've led this with children and with adults. It takes about 15-20 minutes to teach and is easier each week as more and more people join in. A comfortable number to start with is about six or eight people plus leader, and the number will probably double after a few times. All who dance should also join in the singing, at least on the choruses. Singing out the words *Rejoice!* helps the movement to be strong.

Dancing The Lord's Prayer

It is possible for a dance to the *Our Father* to be simple enough for a whole congregation to learn with as much practice as they would normally have for a song (around five minutes). To do this well, the leader should have assimilated the movements beforehand, so that he or she can teach them in a flowing way, and be able to put his or her own soul into the prayer without self-consciousness.

Here is the simple version of an *Our Father* dance. I have taught this more than any other group dance—to children and adults, sitting or standing, in groups of all sizes. (It is always so moving to see a whole group of worshipers bowing and raising arms in praise.)

Opening position: Cross your arms in front of your body and take the hands of the person on either side of you. Still holding hands, bend over and remain in this position for a moment, with a sense of stillness and prayer.

Our Father, who art in heaven, hallowed be thy name; thy kingdom come; thy will be done on earth as it is in heaven. Slowly raise your body and at the same time lift your arms up in a smooth, *continuous* way, holding your neighbors' hands until you naturally let them go as your arms lift higher. (Avoid any pulling.) Uncross your arms (there will be a lovely moment of expansion when everyone does this at the same time) and hold them in an open, praising position, head and chest upraised.

Give us this day our daily bread. Lower your arms, bringing your hands together in a gesture of petition (palms face upward, arms stretched out in front of you about chest height).

And forgive us our trespasses. Bow forward folding your arms to your chest with a sense of contrition.

As we forgive those who trespass against us. Come out of the bow and take the hands of the person on either side of you. (Do not cross your arms this time.)

And lead us not into temptation. Holding hands, all bow deeply.

But deliver us from evil. All raise arms, lifting bodies and heads high.

Priest: "Deliver us, Lord, from every evil . . . " As the celebrant continues praying lower your arms.

For the kingdom, the power, and the glory are yours, now and forever. Amen. All raise arms again, hands still joined.

Joyful Dance With Candles

This dance should combine a sense of reverence with spontaneous joy. Prepare the children ahead of time by discussing with them the beauty of the candle and how they have to hold it so it will not blow out—and how its flickering is like the bouncy spirit of the children themselves—but its innermost point is still yet vibrant, like each one's spirit, warm and filled with unique energy.

This little light of mine, O Lord,
I'm going to let it shine,
This little light of mine, O Lord,
I'm going to let it shine,
This little light of mine, O Lord,
I'm going to let it shine,
Let it shine, let it shine, let it shine.

Children enter from all over the church, walking joyfully, each holding a candle. They converge in front of the altar. All the people in the pews sing and clap.

All over God's kingdom, I'm going to let it shine,
All over God's kingdom, I'm going to let it shine,
All over God's kingdom, I'm going to let it shine,
Let it shine, let it shine, let it shine.

Prepare two leaders beforehand. One leads half the children around the altar to the right, and the other to the left, so that there are two circles moving around the altar, each in different directions. On the last line, all stop and face the altar, raising their candles high.

This little light of mine, O Lord,
I'm going to let it shine,
This little light of mine, O Lord,
I'm going to let it shine,
This little light of mine, O Lord,
I'm going to let it shine,
Let it shine, let it shine, let it shine.

All carefully place candles on altar. As each child comes to the center of the altar, before going back down the aisle, tell him to let his inner light shine in any way he wants, expressing it through movement, with a leap, a turn, a skip, etc. (Adults keep singing and clapping all the way through.)

The originator of these dances is Carla De Sola, a dancer from New York City who contributes a regular column on dance to Liturgy *magazine, and has recently published* Learning Through Dance *(Paulist Press).*

Creating an Environment

Using improvisational theater techniques with groups of children touring the National Collection of Fine Arts in Washington, D.C. led Marjorie Coffey to try similar acting-out methods in her banner and vestment workshops.

What follows is an informal lecture designed for groups of children (and their families) who express an interest in creating their own environment for celebrations. It strives not to provide a comprehensive treatment of the subject: rather it serves as a model—which lends itself easily to adaptation—for the first of a series of workshops in a total parish program devoted to the visual arts.

Have you ever thought about how your body movements convey your mood before you start to talk? When you come home and smell cookies baking, what does it say to you? How does Mother know what kind of day you've had by the way you come up the walk? How does your body talk? . . . What do your shoulders do when you're

cold   hot   frightened   sleepy

or looking for a fight? Shapes and colors can talk without words too.

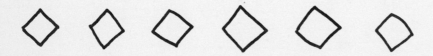

If these squares were people what would they be doing?
     marching in a parade? . . .
     waiting in line at a cafeteria? . . .
Did you ever go into a roomful of strangers? They don't cluster; they stand apart and size each other up first.

What are they doing now? Is it a football huddle? . . . friends at a party? . . .

What happens when a new
shape steps in?

Is he from the other team trying to overhear their signals?

Why do the football teams wear different colored shirts? They did that even before color TV, you know.

Did you ever see someone coming toward you looking very angry . . . a policeman when you were jaywalking . . . a neighbor if your ball broke his window . . . (adults: the driver of the car you hit)? Did you feel like a bug about to be stepped on?

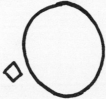

This would be a good time to put the book down and play around with some shapes cut out of paper. Use a contrasting background and see what you can do. Watch the positive and negative space.

Try to squint your eyes and focus on the spaces between the shapes. They should be as interesting (forget beauty for the moment) as the cut shapes.

Think how much you can tell about how people feel about each other by the spaces between them . . . lovers . . . strangers . . . enemies . . . mother and hurt child . . .   Arrange your spaces to convey relationships within a group of shapes as well as between groups.   Think of the sheriff's posse and the outlaws, Christians and lions . . .

LINES tell stories too:

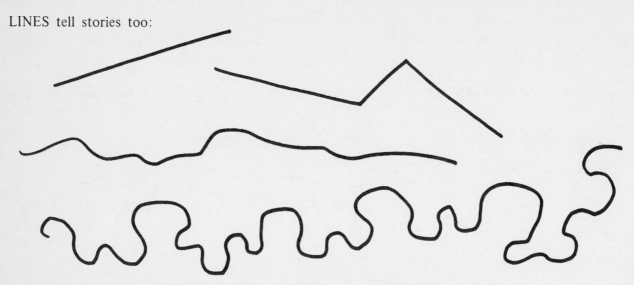

Which road would you take if you were late for dinner?   Which one if you have a new camera to try out?   What state are they crossing, Iowa or West Virginia?   Find some string or yarn and combine lines with your shapes.
  You can fence them in . . . or out . . .

  Let the string wander over your shapes and give them *unity*.

Have you noticed *rhythm* in your designs?
  Try to get some *variety* in size or shape.
  You can make a center of interest (*focus*) by changing just one detail.

If you must put in a word, that would be the place for your message. The eye goes to the odd shape.

If you don't like your results, use these words as a check list for possible flaws . . . Unity . . . Rhythm . . . Variety . . . Focus . . . Balance.

Are you ready to tackle the problems and joys of Color? Get a large stack of colored construction paper and try to make colors work for you. Can you make them . . .

whisper
LAUGH   SHOUT
DANCE   SING

Here are some experiments to try:
1. *Make one color look like two different colors.* Cut two small squares of a light blue gray. Put them in the center of different colors and compare the way they look. Try to find two backgrounds that make them look as though they were cut from different colors of paper. (Hint, see if a dark blue and a bright green will do it)
2. *Make two different colors look the same.* Use one of your blue gray squares and find another sheet of paper close to it but more gray. Try them against a grayed color and a bright color . . . or against a light and a dark background.
3. *Make a piece all the same color appear to darken on one edge and lighten on the other.* Put a color of medium value between one of lighter on one side and one of darker value on the other. The middle color will look darker next to the light piece and lighter on the edge nearer the dark piece. It is called fluting.

As you go through your stack of colored papers begin to think of ways to describe their differences . . .
    warm and cool
    light and dark
    bright or grayed
    heavy or light (weight)

To make a color seem brighter, put it against a grayer background. To make a color seem lighter, put it against a dark background. Remember that it is easier to change colors that are more gray or faded. One of the greatest books ever put together about color is now out in paper back, which is a break as the original, limited edition, portfolio sold for hundreds of dollars. If you want to learn to use color to its utmost limits get Josef Albers' *Interaction of Color*, put out by Yale University Press. (1963) A good book on design is *Basic Design: the Dynamics of Visual Form* by Maurice de Sausmarez (Reinhold Publishing Corporation: New York, 1964).

I think when Jesus invited his listeners to "be as little children" he meant for us to recapture the sense of awe and joy that a child has when (s)he finds a shell on the beach and runs to share the discovery. This is why the painter paints and prophets prophesy . . . to share their visions. Children don't need to have adults cut out patterns for them to follow. They don't need to be told what to draw. They can put shapes and colors together to show how they *feel*, but they freeze up when asked to draw something the adults can recognize as a horse or a person. That is why so many people are afraid to try their hand at art . . . someone has compared their first efforts to Leonardo da Vinci. No one sounds like Van Cliburn the first day he sits at the piano. So try a ban on words, happy smiling faces, and realistic scenes, but let the children (and adults) make their colors dance and shout and pray and

ENJOY!

Burlap is a good way to start; it is cheap, colorful and contrasts well in texture from felt. But respect the integrity of the fabric. It will never be velvet. It will never look like a Bayeux Tapestry. Fringe the edges all around and tie the ones at the top so a chopstick or dowel can slide through. Don't worry about making the fringes neat . . . let them ramble a little.

They will look more alive.

A child believes in miracles because (s)he still has some life-like communication with rocks, shells, dolls, baseball bats, marbles. Look at your pieces of fabric as though they were alive and had friends or enemies, felt more comfortable in some places than in others. Feel in your own muscles the sharp corner of a piece that is too close. If your theme is "Repent" or "Watch Out," then you need to put danger and menace in your banner design. If you want to say "Rejoice," the shapes and colors must dance and sing. If you use words, the shapes and colors of the letters should telegraph the message before there is time to read the words.

Until you are sure of yourself, work with the cheap colored paper and move the cut pieces around at random until a pattern emerges. Then you can shift to the pieces from a rag bag or the small squares of felt from the dime store. Try pinning it together and hanging it where you can see it as you go about your other tasks. Adjust a piece and inch higher or lower; add a piece or take off some if it seems too crowded. Notice how a small piece of a sharply

108

contrasting color can balance the weight of all the other pieces . . . and give the design a punch it lacked before. I sometimes live with a banner for months before I am satisfied enough to sew it together. Don't set deadlines at first until you get acquainted with the possibilities of the materials. Stay loose. Invent new symbols.

Turn banner-making into a party and call in your friends and neighbors. Praying, sharing, breadbreaking, singing may take most of the evening. When the group feels all together the banner may come to life in just a few minutes. Maybe someone wants to take it home to put on the finishing touches.

If the banner goes well try a matching chasuble. The simple, pancho style can be cut out in ten minutes, and felt requires no sewing. Don't let your decorations turn it into a walking sandwich board, but let the colors bring attention to the important actions at the altar. Be sure to check with the celebrant first. If he feels self conscious and uncomfortable he can not do the service well. All our efforts must be to enhance the worship, not to turn it into a carnival.

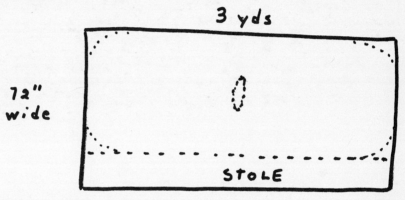

I am a process person; I think that what happens to the group as they work together is as important, perhaps more important, than the product. Quality of workmanship will improve with practice . . . improving our quality of living together as Christians must be practiced too.

BRINGING IT HOME

Letters to Parents

The basic idea behind the Liturgical Conference's Parishes and Families *(published in mid-1973) was that liturgy is not one way of Christian formation among many, but has been and has the possibility of again being the primary school of the biblical faith. Through the keeping of seasons, Sabbaths, special days and ordinary days, faith is communicated not only as things believed or morals condoned but as sharing in a community as well rooted as it is full of variety.*

In the fall of 1973 I had an opportunity to put a bit of this theory into practice with the NOVA community. NOVA is a non-geographical parish across the Potomac from Washington, D.C. For nine weeks I met with the 6 to 8-year-olds in the community for one hour on Sunday mornings.

There were 15 to 25 children each week. The letters which follow were sent through them to their parents. The class was not offered as babysitting or as an answer to religious education, but as an opportunity to give both parents and children some practical ideas. Most of these found their way into the weekly notes to parents.

They were read. And appreciated, I think. Whether or not the basic outlook behind them took root, I don't know. They are printed below in hopes that the approach will be helpful not only as a source of ideas for September, October and November, but as a possible approach—compatible with classes (school or CCD) or with no classes—to a formation program based on resource persons giving help to the home.

—Gabe Huck

September 9

Most of our Sunday meetings will be loosely structured around a theme drawn from the season (and when possible this will relate to the theme of the adult liturgy). They will have only the progression which the season itself has. At our first session our main project will be making a calendar (a giant one) of the days between now and the coming of winter. The themes of the Sundays, birthdays, moons, holidays, special anniversaries, saints' days, will all be on the calendar.

I put a lot of stress on the cycles of days, weeks, years in Christian formation. Everything comes from learning to name the days, observe the Sabbaths, move through and celebrate the seasons. Thus our topics for our meetings will be things like the start of autumn, apples, Halloween, the festival of the saints, death, giving thanks.

Usually our meetings will have songs, stories, activities and some sharing. Through notes like this I will try to keep you informed and offer suggestions that this or that element be put to use in the home during the week as a meal blessing, a good-night, a morning prayer. At the beginning I encourage you to think about the mood or spirit of these months ahead and of the ways it might be fully realized in activities and in signs (rituals, prayers, songs, objects, dances, etc.). What's October all about? November?

Next Sunday, the 16th, is our last summertime meeting. So we will take something that is much a part of the summer: insects. Today I will ask that each child bring an insect (alive, later to be released, if possible). I may be able to get some of the children to volunteer to bring specific insects (your very child may have said, "Oh sure, we have loads of roaches at home!"). A good insect cage is an old piece of screen, formed into a tube, with a clean tuna fish can (top removed) at each end.

If all goes well, we will have learned a special way of singing "Shalom" today. Your child *may* want to teach it to you.

Have a creepy, crawly week! (And this Wednesday is the full harvest moon—celebrate it!)

September 16

Last Sunday we had about 25 children for our first meeting. We learned some names and a song ("Seek and You Shall Find") and a jumping prayer, and made our calendar for the season. Then the time was gone:

This week we're having a last summer meeting with insects, the creatures of summer. The plan is to make a kind of zoo with the insects the children bring, to put up signs, to have some stories, songs and role playing (being grasshoppers, bees, etc.). The idea is to appreciate these creatures, learn to call them brother and sister (we lean on each other, like the song at the liturgy said last week). A couple of good quotes on this:

> Because I am poor
> I pray for every living creature. (Kiowa Indian)

> Brother little fly flies around
> And looks at the sun. (Yaqui Indian)

Most of us have treated bugs as something to be avoided, sprayed, stepped on, swatted, exterminated. Sometimes maybe ok. But Francis and the Indians had it a lot straighter. We'll probably end our session Sunday by sitting down around the insects to share some honey (thanks, bees) which we'll first bless and give thanks for. Then we'll let the insects go.

Perhaps during the week you can make up some prayers with or for the insects. (One thing we may do Sunday is sing "He's got the whole world . . . " putting in different insects—and asking some to act out that insect while we sing.) Or read *Charlotte's Web* (don't be satisfied with the movie!). That can lead right into the arrival of autumn on Saturday, which will be our theme next week.

For next Sunday's meeting I'll ask the children to bring one thing that is a reminder or a creation of the summertime. Something that can be put away now. They won't be bringing it back, so make sure it is something that really is over and done with. Please help them remember. Maybe talk about it.

Did you celebrate the harvest moon last Wednesday? We went with another family to our garden and sang "Praise God from whom all blessings flow . . . ," then we all dug until we found the Alleluia we had buried in a wooden box just before Lent (when we did the first planting). Just as we found it, the moon appeared and we sang an Alleluia. Then the story of the sower informally told. Then we shared some cake and cherry tomatoes (from the garden). Then, because all things are going to fall down soon, we formed a big circle and did ring-around-the-rosie (which was originally a funeral song).

Get ready to welcome autumn.

September 23

The plan for this Sunday is to say farewell to summer and welcome to fall. Those children who were absent last week (or who forgot) will have a chance to make an image of some one thing that summertime this year meant to them and then these will be put with the things others have brought into a box. All will be blessed by the group. Then the box will be closed and we'll try to find a good place outside to bury summertime. If there is time, we will follow this with an old "end of September time" rite—the tug of war. It's really a contest between the forces of autumn and those of summer, so the victors will be named autumn. Then with both sides we'll share a loaf of honey bread.

I would like to explain some of the thinking behind the tug of war and the honey bread. (I believe in a minimum of explaining with the kids—if the things are exciting now and then, what's meant to be communicated will be.) The church now celebrates the feast of angels on September 29, but until recently this was the feast of Michael the Archangel. Why? Michael in Hebrew meant "Who is like God?" He's mentioned in Daniel 10:21 and 12:1 as a warrior on guard over the people. Revelation (12:7) has him leading the forces of heaven against the great dragon. So it was the natural hero's day for this time of year when death and life struggle—celebrating Michael gave hope at the very onset of the cold that life would come back to the earth. So you may want to come up with your own celebration of Michael this coming Saturday. One song we may use is the obvious: "Michael, row your boat ashore . . ." (Use the old verses like: "River is deep and the river is wide, Milk and honey on the other side, Alleluia!")

Rosh Hashonah, the Jewish New Year, begins Wednesday (1 Tishri) at sundown. Some blessings for that night: "Blessed are you, O Lord our God, Ruler of the whole world, who has kept us alive, and upheld us, and enables us to reach this season." Or: "May it be your will, O Lord our God and God of our fathers and mothers, to renew for us a happy and sweet year." That last goes with the custom of dipping fruits and breads in honey as the sun goes down and the new year begins. (Thus our honeycake.) The feast of Yom Kippur, the greatest Jewish holy day, the day of atonement, will occur on October 6. Perhaps you can talk with someone or read about its meaning and observance.

When we meet on October 7 we will celebrate two saints: Francis of Assisi (who died on October 4, 1226) and Woody Guthrie (who died October 3, 1967). Maybe you know Francis's poems about Brother Sun and Sister Death and all the family. Woody knew about the family too. Maybe your family can sing his song "This land is your land. . . . " And here is a verse he wrote for it that you don't hear too often:

As I was walking along that highway
I saw a sign that said "No Trespassing"
But on the other side, it didn't say nothing—
That side was made for you and me.

Have you learned to pray "Shalom" with singing and gestures yet?

October 7

Between now and Advent many of our meetings will be about our ancestors. During November this will be a celebration of all the heroes and saints and another about death itself. This month begins Sunday with two persons who died during the first week of October: Francis of Assisi in 1226 and Woody Guthrie in 1967.

The autumn time is for thinking about where we have been, who we have been. And part of this is the naming of our saints. Now no one in the past ever had to solve our problems, no one had to prove he or she could be a decent human being in times like these. But I believe that one of the reasons living is so hard for many of us is that we were seldom offered (and seldom discovered on our own) people of the past who could help, seldom got to know these people through stories and through celebrations that made their special spark our own. Yet our religious tradition is much involved with this approach. The way of naming God was by naming the ancestors: "the God

116

of Abraham, Isaac and Jacob"—and of Sarah, Rebekah and Rachel. That brought it home. That is why we might name God concretely: the God of Francis and Woody. But then you have to know their stories.

This 6 to 8-year-old time seems to be a good one for the telling of these stories. If you do that well, and make some efforts to see that the heroes live on in you, you've surely done religious education for your children. I might share with you a couple of ways from our family. We use the Liturgical Conference calendar and often on an anniversary of someone we want to *remember*, some words of that person and an appropriate song form the prayer before the evening meal. Looking ahead far enough, a good book can be found from the children's department of the library, and become the evening story. A more important thing for us has been continuing family reading when we are all together at breakfast. We read last year some biography (Helen Keller, Black Elk) then found Laura Ingalls Wilder's books and have been reading them for almost a year (we're on the eighth volume, only two more slim books to go and all of us dread finishing). The special meaning of these stories is that our great-grandparents were settling in the plains at the same time as the Wilder and the Ingalls families, so we can feel that the story is very much our own.

If you want to find out about Francis with your children, there are lots of biographies. Sophie Jewett's *God's Troubadour* is easy and interesting. Our kids especially love the story of Francis and the wolf of Gubbio. There are wonderful records of Woody Guthrie singing and of others singing his children's songs ("Songs To Grow On"). His autobiography is *Bound for Glory*; another book of his stories and poems is *Born To Win*, and Henrietta Yurchenco's *A Mighty Hard Road* is a short biography. Some libraries will have the records as well as a two-record concert of tribute to Woody with Dylan, Baez, Odetta, Seeger and others. These two, Woody and Francis—hoboes, poets, singers—are two of the most interesting people you could ever meet

Next week is apple time and harvest figure time. Please help your child remember to bring some one article of old clothing (child's or adult's) that you don't want back, and something of the autumn (a sack of leaves, some acorns, corn stalks, etc.). Johnny Appleseed might be the story—several good biographies of him are available at libraries. Maybe you should go to an apple festival this year.

October 14

Today is an apple-time harvest celebration. The things I asked the children to bring (a discarded piece of clothing, a bag of leaves or acorns or such) will be used to make a harvest figure. (With scarecrows and snowmen—or snowpeople—harvest figures are pictured in a wonderful book called *Ephemeral Folk Figures*; beautiful photos.) Some lucky one of you will be able to take the harvest figure home after your child wins it.

For stories, we are thinking about *The Giving Tree* by Shel Silverstein, and/or

Johnny Appleseed. John Chapman got the name Appleseed from the people he knew on the American frontier in the early 19th century. He spent a lifetime walking from place to place, planting the apple trees, preaching, doing good, making peace between Indians and settlers. The kind of hero we could use more of. And apples are one of the most beautiful of all the things we take for granted. This is the month when our part of the country is filled with the many varieties; perhaps this could be the year when you get to know a few by name and shape and color and taste. Maybe have an all apple meal: cider, butter, sauce, pie. Make up some poems about apples: seeds, core, peel, stem. Sing: "Don't sit under the apple tree. . . . "

Harvest festivals are times of giving thanks. Sometimes giving thanks is more boasting than humble ("I give you thanks that I am not like the rest of men . . . " or as: "We give you thanks that we have plenty to eat," in other words, that we're not like the rest of the world). The biblical notion of giving thanks wasn't that way. It was the same idea as blessing (the stories of the last supper show this as Jesus takes the bread and then the wine). We might move towards a better way of living with creation (not above it, exploiting it, indifferent to it) if we got to be better blessers. The Jewish form of blessing can be fine: "Blessed art thou, O Lord our God, Ruler of the Universe, for you have given us the fruit of the vine." Or in this case: " . . . for you have given us the fruit of the apple tree." While blessing the food or anything else, hold the hands out over as a gesture of your presence, your own self being shared with the thing blessed.

Next week, though it is only October 21, will be our last meeting before Halloween. But since that day is so important in the lives of children, we can begin getting ready for it (I'll bet most have anyway). Halloween pre-dates Christianity. In one way or another the days of long darkness and the death of so much in nature led peoples to a day (or night) of ghosts and spirits and witches (for witches, it is still a big day). I don't think it is just the treats that turn kids on to this day (most of them have enough of that in the ordinary course of events). Part of it is the dressing up, being some-one other than yourself. For next Sunday, please have your child bring the makings of a mask (head-size paper sack, for sure, and then whatever you can imagine: maybe yarn or buttons or raffia or bits of material—you and the child go through the family junk). Some children will forget so send a few extra things if you're a rememberer.

October 21

Where did Halloween come from? "Once the harvest dancing and feasting was over, man often found himself beset by fears. Suppose something should happen to the stored food. Suppose the children were to fall ill, or the cattle die. With the winter's hard-got rations stored under his roof, man felt vulnerable. Evil, destructive spirits, envious of his comfort, might seek to destroy him. Bad witches, goblins and demons were thought to roam the countryside; the souls of the dead were believed to rise from the ground seeking shelter among living men. Evil spirits must be purged and scared away if men were to survive the approaching winter. Again fire was used to drive unwanted specters from the community. Not long ago in Northern Europe every house had its fire built nearby on All Hallow's Eve; in earlier times, fires on the same date marked the Druid Samhain. There was no gleeful dancing around these fires. Since evil spirits would try to grab anyone they found roaming about, people carried torches after dark and disguised themselves with masks and costumes. Ceremonies, chants and charms were devised to ward off the baleful influence of the evil spirits." (From *Celebrate The Sun* by Betty Nickerson, p. 73.)

Various peoples seem to have done it various ways, but nearly everywhere there were ways to mark what seemed the death of the sun. The bonfires were lighted to help the sun, to carry on sun's work. New hearth fires, to be kept lighted all winter, were started by the heads of households, each taking a piece of the community's great bonfire on this day (the kind of ritual communion we could all use more of). In general this was a time (especially this one night) when the dead came back to warm themselves, possibly to feast— and the living were scared. People made masks so they would become someone else; they did things together because it was too scary to be alone at such a time; they kept the torches handy because we all know how much light helps when we are frightened. It was a festival of the people and it did not cease being so when the people, as church, celebrated the dead at this time of year with the festivals of all the saints and souls. (Some of the customs that carried over seem especially helpful for coming to terms with the dead: as the practice of taking the favorite foods of those who have died to the graveyard and the ritual feasting there.) Most of the things we are talking about here—the fears of the unknown, the uncertainty about the dead, the need to temporarily stop being oneself and for a night at least put on a mask and be somebody different—these things aren't that much different for us today. Only thing is, we don't know what to do with them.

I grew up in a town of about 10,000 in Nebraska. Every year on October 31 we had what was called Hallowesta. The schools and offices closed. The streets were closed to traffic all day. Anyone seen in the downtown area without a costume on was liable to be hauled before the kangaroo court and publicly imprisoned (this happened to my father once and I was terrified). There were various parades, awards, giveaways, prizes, contests—a whole day climaxing in a nighttime parade with floats and bands. Everyday life came to a complete stop. The most powerful and the least were no different— if anything, the former was the greater fool. Something ended and we were ready for winter. There were many good things about this festival, but one shouldn't be missed: it wasn't just something for the kids—it was for everybody.

So why not, for your Halloween this year, all of you make costumes or masks? Work together or do it separately and then scare and surprise each other. (And how about a few good tricks? If the goblins won't do it, we can help them out!) The bonfire has been replaced by the candle in the pumpkin, but let this be a celebration of light (there will be little if any moon that night).

119

Light candles while everyone tells ghost stories. Maybe you have no relations buried nearby, but there are plenty of cemeteries for visiting, singing, praying (you won't be bothered), maybe picnicking.

Other family parts of Halloween might be doing a little something to keep this from being just another consumer feast. Talk together about a treat to give the visiting children that is both fun, well liked, and not junk. Impossible? We gave big handfuls of peanuts last year and kids loved them. The UNICEF collection is also a good way to keep the feast.

Books. Most books on holidays are in the 394.269 section of the library. A typical one that's helpful is Marjorie Krythe's *All About American Holidays*. A good children's book that explains the history and customs is *A Holiday Book—Halloween* by Lillie Peterson. We may learn in class Sunday a chant she gives for trick or treating from the past:

> Soul, soul, an apple or two,
> If you haven't an apple, a pear wil do,
> An apple or a pear, or a plum or a cherry,
> Any good thing to make us merry.
> One for Peter, Two for Paul,
> Three for the man who made us all.
> Up with the kettle and down with the pan.
> Give us good alms and we'll be gone.

There are a number of good books on mask making. *Masks and Mask Makers* by Kari Hunt and Bernice Wells Carlson; *Mask Making* by Matthew Baranski; *Masks* by C. J. Alkenci; *Funny Bags* by Betsy Pflug; *Folding Paper Masks* by Shari Lewis.

Plan with the children the schedule for Halloween and the following day or days. Come up with ways to keep it from being a who-can-get-the-most-candy-and-eat-it-quickest night by planning ahead as to where the goodies will be stored after the trick or treat, and how they will be used for snacks and desserts during the coming week.

November 4

This Sunday we will be doing some celebrating of heroes. I have in mind now dividing into groups of three, in each a 6, a 7, and an 8-year-old. Each group could make its list of heroes: real, fictitious, imaginary, dead and alive. After sharing the lists and perhaps taking a try at "When the Saints Go Marching In" (with rhythm instruments if we get some together in time), we'll have a "hero" story or two, then make some puppets of the heroes.

The festival of All Saints and the November emphasis on the dead was but a church emphasis on what people had been doing with this time of year. After the harvest came the fears—shorter days, colder, death all around in nature. One aspect of this is a concentration on death itself and we will talk some about that next week. (But you might be thinking about how important and pervasive it is and how few good rituals, myths or anything else we have that prepare us to die or deal with death.) Another aspect was the emphasis on the saints and heroes, the great ones who were among the dead. The ancestors whose virtues are told in the legends are held before us, not only as some kind of moral model, but as a partial explanation of who we are, where we are, where we might be going. Like the song says: "We are walking in the footsteps of those who've gone before, and we'll all be reunited. . . . "

So use November as a time to talk with children about heroes and ancestors and saints. At some ages they have more of a thing for heroes than at others, but there's always a willingness to hear a good story. Some of these can be about your own childhood, about your parents when you were young, the story of how they came to live where they did, the occupations, what part of this country or other countries their parents came from. Maybe you could start to do a family tree—names, places, birth and death years—whatever you may know. Next week send it with the children and we'll talk about them. Some of our parents talked about their family background a lot, but many did not. For various reasons the latter wanted to live in the present and so left us a generation that knows very little about roots. It is getting so common for people in their 30's and 40's to be searching out old aunts and uncles to try to find out what the family was like back then. Do some of this if you need to. Gather pictures and other memorabilia for a November display. Trace on a map the moving about of the various families that came together to make your family. Sing some of the favorite songs of parents or grandparents. Eat some of the foods that were favorites of previous generations. Maybe this is a good way to work up to Thanksgiving. Construct your own litany of the saints.

November 11

Last week we talked a little about family trees and most of the children seemed quite interested. Why not do one at home during the rest of November? One way is to use pictures of as many relations as possible (that means a large piece of posterboard for the whole tree). It not only gives a good sense of time (with the birth and death dates) and place (if you note where each came from and settled) but also relationships (what's an uncle? a cousin? etc.). Maybe you can trace some shared characteristics, physical and otherwise, too. We have talked in class about the stories that are handed down in families—why not try to recall some of these and retell them?

The class for Sunday looks something like this. The subject is death. As I have said, it is so much a part of our experience, of our personality—yet as Christians right now we have not got strong rituals for dealing with it. Instead, we leave it to a confused society. So, using a story or two, we will move from talk of the family trees, to talk of death. Finally we will bless and share some donuts. The donut, according to legend, originated with talk of death and saints: when the rich would go out to church on All Saints they would leave their homes open and food on the tables; the poor were expected to enter and enjoy. But then some of the rich got worrying about the souls of the poor and invented the donut—the shape was to remind the poor, as they ate, of eternity.

I think a good part of our task (for ourselves and children) is to get closer to a world where things do die. We have isolated ourselves from nature, put the dying away. Most encounter death only in accidents, wars and other unnatural ways—no contact with death as the natural part of a cycle. Within nature, that cycle is annual and helps us select this time of year as the most natural to deal with death through story and ritual and meditation and preparation. November of each year might be the time to take another look at your will and burial plans. Maybe plan your own funeral and revise it each year. Litanies of saints and ancestors might be a good prayer for the month with responses like: "Congratulations! The whole world awaits your return!" (from the *Washington Free Press* when Ho Chi Minh died) or "This world was lucky to see him (her) born!" (from a lovely Woody Guthrie song about FDR). Other good songs would be "Swing Low," and the refrain "Will the circle be unbroken . . . " (that goes with the donuts!).

Finally, three excellent stories to use with children in this age range. *The Tenth Good Thing About Barney* by Judith Viorst, *Annie and The Old One* by Miska Miles, and *Growing Time* by Sandol Stoddard Warburg. Other simple ideas would include lighting candles at the dinner table for all friends, relations or personal saints who have died in the past year (in this past week Dr. Ginott and John Niehardt, who wrote *Black Elk Speaks*, have died—not bad saints to have.)

These letters were written by Gabe Huck, editor of Liturgy, *the membership journal of the Liturgical Conference. Gabe has given numerous workshops on children's and family celebrations and is presently serving as director of adult education and youth activities in Sacred Heart Parish, Yankton, South Dakota.*

Some Signs, Songs and Stories

"Our prayer ought to be short...

. . . and pure, unless it happens to be prolonged by inspiration of divine grace. In community, however, let prayer be very short."–St. Benedict

The factor of time–the duration or length of a celebration–is a very significant one in the planning of ritual or prayer events which involve children. An overlong service, despite the quality of all of its parts, is in grave danger of losing its total effect or experience value.

What follows is a sampling of ideas: elements (a few songs, a few stories, a few signs) around which liturgies can be created, as well as some sample celebrations. In a few instances, the models provided are fairly long; users of the volume are urged to study them for the direction they give in terms of "putting the pieces together"–and not as guides to be slavishly followed. The chief function of this section is to invite and encourage planners to expand their notions of what an appropriate "source" for a celebration is. Anything and everything belongs in our storehouse–the old and the new, the sacred and the profane, the childlike and the not-so-childlike. Our treasury knows no strangers save the unbeautiful and the untrue.

Advent

On the day before the first Sunday of Advent, make a family advent calendar with something behind each new day. Or make candles and gather objects for an advent wreath. Or find a fallen branch, set it firmly in sand and call it an advent tree upon which a new promise is hung each day by one member of the family (Advent is a season of promise). Or gather symbols of things to fear and make a mobile. Make a list of the advent songs you want to sing and the stories you want to read.

Feast of Lights

What follows is a Christian adaptation of the festival of Chanukah for use in the home. Chanukah (or Hannukah) comes in December–Advent on the church's calendar. It commemorates the cleansing of the Temple in 169 B.C. after the revolt of Judah Maccabee and his brothers drove out the Hellenistic rulers.

We are told that in the time of the Roman persecution the Jews would keep gambling games around when they met to pray or study Torah. In this way if a Roman official should happen upon them and want to know why so many Jews were gathered together they could claim to be merely gambling. For this reason Chanukah is one of great merriment and should be celebrated with the playing of games.

The rite below was adapted by Frederick E. Jessett. He describes it by saying "the rite lasts for nine days rather than the traditional eight, with the final day's candle being lighted for John the Baptist. The only supplies needed for the service are a menorah and forty-six candles that fit it. Since you are supposed to watch the candle until it burns down, small ones are an advantage. Each night new candles are used and burned down. You will use one the first night, two the second and so on until you have burned a total of forty-five plus one or two used as lighters for the others. A menorah can be purchased; it can also be made from clay or wood or from discarded pieces of tin, shaped and with holes punched to fit the candles. (The one long part of the service all say together can be lettered on a large, colorful paper so that all can read from one place.)"

In the evening, the family is gathered around or before the menorah. All lights are out. Before lighting the candle(s), the mother says this blessing:

"Blessed are you, O Lord our God, King of the universe: You have sanctified us by your commandments, and commanded us to kindle the light of Chanukah.

"Blessed are you, O Lord our God, King of the universe: You wrought miracles for our fathers in days of old at this season."

(On the first night only, she says the following blessing: "Blessed are you, O Lord our God, King of the universe: You have kept us in life and preserved us, and enabled us to reach this season.")

After the mother has lighted the candle(s), all say together: "We kindle these lights on account of the miracles, the deliverance, and the wonders which you did for our fathers, by means of your holy priests. During all the eight days of Chanukah these lights are sacred, neither is it permitted to us to make any profane use of them, but we are only to look at them, in order that we may give thanks to your name for your miracles, your deliverance and your wonders."

Then the father will say: "Tonight we light a candle for the prophet_____ , who left this message from the Lord."

Then he will read the lesson appointed as follows:
First night: *Amos.* Amos 5:6-15, 21-24
Second night: *Hosea.* Hosea 2:18-20; 11:1-4
Third night: *Joel.* Joel 2:12-14*a*, 28; 3:14-18*a*

126

Fourth night: *Isaiah.* Isaiah 7:14; 9:2-7; 11:1-9
Fifth night: *Jeremiah.* Jeremiah 31:7-14, 31-34
Sixth night: *Ezekiel.* Ezekiel 37:1-14
Seventh night: *Poet of the Exile.* Isaiah 40:1-11; 60:1-3; 61:1-9
Eighth night: *Malachi.* Malachi 2:10; 3:1; 4:2-5
Ninth night: *John the Baptist.* John 1:6-8, 19-37.

Of course the lessons for each day may be lengthened or shortened according to need and interest. Pertinent songs can be added as desired. It might be helpful to review the names of the prophets from the previous evenings each night.

If the candles are not burned down after the lesson is read, the family could engage in conversation with one another while watching the lights burn down. Talk might even center around the meaning of the prophet's message for today.

The mother's part could be taken by a daughter on certain evenings, and the father's by a son. However, it should be remembered that the lighting of the Chanukah lights, as also the Sabbath lights, is done always by a woman of the household.

A Parish Advent Celebration

As the people arrive, they are greeted, coats taken, and all are directed to an unrolled length of newsprint that stretches along the floor of the parish hall until, halfway to the back, it leaves the floor to rest on a couple of long church-type tables. Where the paper leaves the floor for the tables, there is a large, dead tree branch held upright in a pail of rocks. Tied to all the extremities of the branch are dozens of beautiful apples.

All along the length of the newsprint are scattered crayons. People are invited to draw themselves on the paper. Adults could work at the tables if they wish, children on the floor. (No bystanders allowed!) As this is taking place, a song is being sung by a group on the stage area of the hall. One by one the children and adults move from the paper to the singing. The words can be written large on posters and hung above the singers. The song: "Bring Me a Rose"—new verses might be made up for the occasion.

Next, all are invited to sit on the floor and listen to the first reading—from the Book of Isaiah:
> But a shoot shall sprout from the stump of Jesse,
>   and from his roots a bud shall blossom.
> The spirit of the Lord shall rest upon him:
>   a spirit of wisdom and of understanding . . . (11:1-9)

Response: the singing of the round, "I am a poor man, nothing do I have, I will give my heart." A simple gesture can be taught for each line (arms crossed over chest, moving to arms extended downwards with open palms, moving to hands touching heart).

When the words and gestures are learned, all move away from the stage area to surround the tree and the mural of self-portraits. Here all can sing the song through several times with gestures—as a round.

The blessing of the apples, the drawings and each other. Everyone extends their arms in a gesture of blessing while the reader prays:
> We praise you, Father, for the gift of apples, Staymans and Winesaps and Delicious and Jonathans. And for the gift of trees like the Giving Tree: for shade and wood and fruit and climbing and beauty and rest. We praise you for this Christmas time of gift-giving when we try to make and create and find things to give others. We need to be poor people so we can give ourselves in all our gifts, all these little folks we have drawn on the paper here. We praise you for Jesus who gave the blind sight, the deaf sound and the poor a friend. Amen.

All sit down in place and listen to a record ("I'd Like to Teach the World to Sing," or some other appropriate song). Now all are asked to speak out their own Christmas wishes in the form, "I'd like to give _____ a _____." (the world some peace, mother a washing machine—anything and everything). All stand, join hands and recite the Our Father together.

Next the children are invited to come and take the apples from the tree and share them with their families and the other adults in the group. After a few moments of eating and visiting, everyone is asked to form the circle and hold up the apple cores. The leader prays:
> Thank you, Father, for the apple cores and apple seeds and for all the seeds that are waiting to come to life, like we are, like Jesus was. Amen.

Closing song: "O Come, O Come, Emmanuel."

Christmas Eve

A day for preparing the special foods, the gifts, the tree (perhaps a live one that can be planted afterwards) . . . and a night for sitting down together to tell the story and sing and light candles.

It might be good to intersperse the nativity story with some other lines, a narrative that speaks not only of Jesus' birth, but of his life: why he was different from other men. A few excerpts from the play, *Jesus Christ Lawd T'day*, follow—the creation of the Black American Theatre of Washington, D.C.

"That was a cold night, the night you was born, way out in the country yonder, in the barn with them beasts. My man, he covered us over with his great wool coat, and went and sat out in the yard, under the stars."

"He had a strange way with him, my son; always had, from the day he first come. His eyes . . . they was wonderful. They held folk. That and his tongue and his tender pitiful heart. They didn't understand it down here. None of us understood it. We was blind—even me. Many a time I got in his way and tried to hinder him. I was afraid for him, ashamed. And then he'd look at me . . . They was always wonderful, his eyes."

"He wasn't particular, my son. He would go with anybody. He loved them so. There wasn't a drunken bibber in the place, not a thief, not a loose woman on the streets, but called him brother. He would eat with them, drink with them, go to their parties. He would go with grand folk, too; gentlemen. He wasn't particular. He would go with anybody."

Or perhaps, if excitement is running very high, and listening to more than the "story" is too much to ask of the children, a short, simple quote might be read by one of the youngsters before gifts are opened—especially if they have been encouraged to make some of their presents. These lines from Emerson are nice: "Rings and jewels are not gifts, but apologies for gifts. The only gift is a portion of thyself . . . Therefore the poet brings his poem; the shepherd, his lamb; the farmer, corn; the miner, a gem; the sailor, coral and shells . . . "

Epiphany

A day for blessing the rooms of the home. Some do this by moving from room to room and marking with chalk above each door:

$$19+C+M+B+75$$

The letters stand for the three kings: Caspar, Melchior and Baltassar.
Those who join the little procession might stop in each room, get the feel/ smell/sight/sound, recall something that happened there, make a plan. "Visit this home, O Lord. Drive far from it all snares of the enemy. Let your holy angels live here with us, and let your blessing be always upon us. Amen."

"Nothing Left to Fear"

A lenten celebration, for a family, or groups of families, or a class. If the closing rite is used, the service will have to be held out-of-doors.

Planners of lenten liturgies should look to the seasonal change in their part of the country, their particular urban or rural setting and ask what signs there are that can be shown, sung about, watched, listened to, smelled: simple things that contain within themselves a kind of progression. The movement through Lent, toward Easter is the movement of these signs of the springtime.

Song: "Sunshine Man" or "New Morning" (Bob Dylan)

THE STORY OF LUCY LIGHT

"Mr. Sun wakes up later and later every day! Brother Lars does not have enough light for milking the cow, and father must chop wood in the dark. Mother can't do her spinning, and I can't tell if winter's first snow has fallen!"

(The children might be encouraged to do gestures as the story is told, or read, to them . . . here, waking up, milking a cow, chopping wood, spinning, etc.)

All Sweden was covered with night, and everybody was glum and gloomy. Lucy decided everyone needed a good breakfast to cheer them up.

Lucy woke early, baked a batch of ginger cookies, and brewed a pot of coffee. Then she heard the faint tapping of heavy, moist snowflakes against the window pane (*gesture of faint, steady tapping*), and she dashed outside to smile at the winter sky. She sang and danced under a shower of falling snow-flakes and shooting stars until her hair glimmered with melting snow and the dazzle of the starlight.

Even Mr. Sun peeked over the horizon, a bit earlier than usual, to see what was happening (*hands shading eyes, or whatever the children feel is a good gesture*). He saw Lucy dance back indoors, and through the window he saw her serve hot cookies and strong coffee to smiling Lars, and her cheerful mother and father.

All through winter, Mr. Sun awoke earlier and earlier just to watch Lars smile and listen to little Lucy sing. The days got longer and longer and SOON IT WAS SPRING!

Response: (sung to any familiar melody)
> Lucy light, Lucy bright:
> Shortest day, longest night!

Leader:
All good things have beginnings and ends . . . and in-betweens. The season of Lent takes six weeks to happen—when the dark and cold and sadness of winter slowly turn into springtime. That is what Lent means: springtime. IT'S GETTING LIGHTER!

All:
"Morning after morning he opens my ear that I may hear . . . "

Leader:
IT'S GETTING WARMER!

All:
" . . . for you who fear my name, there will arise the sun of justice with its healing rays."

Leader:
EVERYTHING IS GROWING.

All:
"It is the smallest seed of all, yet it becomes so big . . . that the birds of the sky come and build their nests in its branches."

Leader:
AND THE SEED FALLS ASLEEP SO THAT IT CAN BRING NEW LIFE.

All:
"Unless the grain of wheat falls to the earth and dies, it remains just a grain of wheat. But if it dies, it produces much fruit."

Leader:
To his servants humble and lowly, he comes and brings with him a great new life. Thus he shows in every generation love and kindness toward all his friends.

The celebration concludes with a simple ritual: All are invited to stamp on the earth, beat it with sticks, make loud noises to rouse the sleeping spirit of springtime. The leader might begin a hymn—"Lift Every Voice and Sing" (facing the rising sun of our new day begun, let us march on till victory is won) or some other appropriate song.

Lent/Reconciliation

A liturgy of reconciliation might begin with participants assigned to one of four groups. Each group receives a box containing the broken or torn pieces of something—in one a large ceramic platter, in another a large ceramic vase or cup, in the third a table, and in the last a loose coat or poncho. Each group also receives the glue (fast-drying), or hammer and nails, or needles, pins and thread that they need.

In this way they act out the meaning of "reconciliation," i.e., putting things back together that *belong together, reestablishing the whole* which cannot function properly in separate pieces. This activity is woven into a liturgy of the word. When the work is complete, the four groups bring their "offerings" together where the platter (paten), cup (chalice), table (altar) and coat (vestment) are made ready for the celebration of the eucharist which can follow immediately or at a later time.

Another lenten celebration (or series of celebrations) can be built around the theme of the talents—a positive approach to the business of self-examination. *The Three Robbers* is a children's book by Tomi Ungere (Atheneum) in which the treasure (talents, gifts, potential) lying unused in the castle is discovered by a young girl (grace, the Holy Spirit) who helps the Robbers (us) use it for

131

good. The book is far more lighthanded and enjoyable than this synopsis might indicate. Children love the story, in book form or as a filmstrip (from Weston Woods). It is a good preparation for, and contemporary parallel to, the biblical parable of the talents. (Cf. Luke 19:11-17.)

Lent/New Year/Graduation

"The disciples were on the road going up to Jerusalem, with Jesus walking in the lead. Their mood was one of wonderment, while that of those who followed was fear. Taking the Twelve aside once more, he began to tell them what was going to happen to him. 'We are on our way up to Jerusalem, where the Son of Man will be handed over to the chief priests and the scribes. They will condemn him to death and hand him over to the Gentiles, who will mock him and spit at him, flog him, and finally kill him. But three days later he will rise.'" (Mark 10:32-34)

We feel the wonderment of those early disciples, the fear of those who followed Jesus on his journey to Jerusalem. We feel the mystery of what lies ahead, and face the unknown with both attraction and dread. Children are endowed with boundless optimism, yet at the same time, recognize that sacrifices of some kind will be expected of them as part of growing up. The dragons will have to be slain, the glass mountain will have to be scaled, the enchanted forest penetrated. Jesus had to make his journey too . . . and the evangelists develop the symbol of the "journey to Jerusalem" to represent the courage and determination with which Jesus answered the call and followed the guidance of his Father.

It would be a very suitable theme on which to build a liturgy for the new year, for Lent, or for a graduation—times when we look back at what we have done and become, and look forward with new determination, courage, and hope because Jesus has, after all, promised to walk with us on our Journey to Jerusalem.

Readings:
Matthew 10:7-8; 10:38-39; 16:21
Luke 9:51; 10:1
Acts 13:47
"A young man, adamant in his committed life . . . " (Dag Hammarskjöld, *Markings*)
"Cheshire-Puss," she began, rather timidly . . . "Would you tell me, please, which way I ought to go from here?"
"That depends a good deal on where you want to get to," said the Cat.
"I don't much care where . . . " said Alice.
"Then it doesn't matter which way you go," said the Cat. (Lewis Carroll, *Alice's Adventures in Wonderland*)

Signposts along the journey:
"For all that has been—Thanks!
To all that shall be—Yes!"—Hammarskjöld

"Man was designed with legs, not roots."—Buckminster Fuller

"Let us send men ahead to explore the land and report to us on the road we must follow and the cities we must take. They set out and explored and reported, 'The land which the Lord our God gives us is good.' "—based on Dt 1:22-25

Another New Year/Graduation Celebration

A celebration of "hopes for the future" might include the construction of a calendar of what might or ought to happen. The congregation, upon gathering, receive large squares of paper, each of which represents a "day" or an event. Felt pens are also available. Each person works on one or more "days" using words and/or pictures to note the celebration of his hoped-for event.

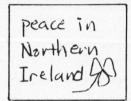

These are brought in procession to a large (*very* large) sheet of paper or fabric designed to represent a calendar, and hanging within the view of the community. A representative of the congregation (if it is a large group) receives each "day" and announces it to the congregation, which responds in unison, "Whatever you ask the Father, he will give you in my name" (Jn 16:23), or another appropriate response. It is then taken by helpers who pin or tape it quickly to the calendar. This rite constitutes the "prayer of the faithful." The presider summarizes all of these hopes in a prayer.

The song "Turn, Turn, Turn" would be appropriate during this liturgy.

Palms to Ashes

The services of Palm Sunday remind Christians of their predecessors who first acclaimed Jesus as messiah and king. How would *we* welcome a new ruler, a new president? With ticker tape, with confetti, with campaign posters on sticks, with flags. Children can make and carry their own campaign posters and banners for Jesus, in addition to the traditional palms, in the Palm Sunday procession. These posters, banners and flags could then be collected, along with the palms, and saved for the liturgy of Ash Wednesday.

The acclamation of the people on Palm Sunday was misguided—not in having Jesus as its object, but in expecting him to assume the direct guidance of the state. That hope was dashed when he was arrested, tried and executed. Those whose interest in Jesus had been limited to what they could get from him rather than how he could help them change their lives, deserted their "candidate" in a hurry, discarding the palms with which they had greeted him a short time before. The burning of the palms as the opening ceremony on Ash Wednesday is a fitting symbol of all the false hopes which went "up in smoke" when Jesus revealed himself as a suffering servant rather than a politician/king.

We all harbor false hopes for God—we want him to "be good to us" in return for our homage . . . we want our virtue rewarded with good grades, a new bicycle, popularity at school . . . we expect our national democratic virtues to bring blessings of prosperity, world prominence and special guidance for our political leaders. The palms, confetti and campaign posters being burned can symbolize once again that Jesus will not allow himself to become identified with particular countries or political aspirations, or the narrow material aims of any group or individual.

Passover-Holy Thursday

A night for preparing and eating together the Seder: the lamb, the unleavened bread, the bitter herb, the wine. Or a number of families might eat together, each preparing one of the traditional foods and each child and adult sharing in the asking of questions and the telling of the long story of man's movement from slavery to freedom.

"Lo! This is the bread of affliction which our ancestors ate in the land of Egypt. Let all who are hungry eat thereof; and all who are in need come and celebrate the Passover.

"Why is this night different from all other nights?

"Because we were slaves unto Pharaoh in Egypt, and the Lord our God brought us forth from thence, with a mighty hand, and an outstretched arm.

"It was not our ancestors only that the Most Holy, blessed be he, redeemed from Egypt, but us also did he redeem with them."—from *The Freedom Seder* by Arthur Waskow.

Good Friday

"Time passed; on a season he sprang from the ground, swarmed a tall tree and arms balancing wide beautifully grappled the tree till he died of the love in his heart like a ruinous wound."—John of the Cross

Easter Sunday

A day to celebrate the new life of Jesus Christ and of the earth at springtime. A day for watching the sun rise and making it welcome, for feeling the earth warm with us. A day for shouting messages and confusion and excitement like that of Jesus' friends. A day for wearing Easter bonnets and parading. A day for celebrating flowers and honoring eggs.

A Celebration of the Spirit

(For possible use as preparation for confirmation . . . or a liturgy during the season of Pentecost.)

PEOPLE ENTER: A tape of wind sounds is playing. A table, placed just inside the room, contains dozens of nails of all sizes and many pieces of thread. Above the table are several coat hangers, and to these the children attach nails as they enter; this makes a lovely set of wind-chimes.

Another table is in the center of the room. On it is a large glass bowl half filled with pure olive oil. On the olive oil are a number of lighted wicks, each inserted through a cork to keep it floating upright with the bottom of the wick in the oil. These burn throughout the celebration and, since the room is fairly dark, make the only bright light available. (A single overhead light is used, and put out at the time of the blessing and anointing.)

A circle of chairs is set up around the table, far enough back so that all the activities can go on.

INTRODUCTION AND WELCOME: The leader invites the children to enjoy this time when they are all together. He then asks everyone to do a simple circle dance to the music being played ("Dueling Banjos," a theme from *Deliverance*): the legs are kept stiff and are kicked forward, alternating right and left in time to the music. Two minutes of this are exhausting . . . all are almost ready to collapse on the final note!

STORY: Next, the story of Elijah when he too was winded, ready to give up his spirit, in fact, and instead was ordered to go out to Mount Horeb and wait for the Lord. The Lord came to him not in the storm, the fire or the earthquake, but in the gentle breeze.

RESPONSE: Everyone stands and reaches high into the air to jump as high as possible three times—each time shouting louder the traditional word addressed to the Spirit, "Come!" The children remain standing as Judy Collins's recording of "Simple Gifts" is played. (The song is an obvious choice to emphasize how simple are the gifts which are given and received in celebrations of our faith: water, bread, wine, oil, salt, ashes, earth, the gestures of blessing, forgiving, loving.)

CHORAL READING: As the group sits down, each person is given a script for the choral reading. The parts are numbered, and each copy of the script is marked with the part number to be read by the person holding it. In addition to the single parts, there are lines to be read by the whole group.

The reading is an assembly of scripture texts about the wind and breath of the Lord: the creation, the wind after the flood, the wind over the sea on the way out of Egypt, Elisha breathing into the mouth of the dead child, Ezekiel and the bones, Daniel and the coming days of the spirit, stories of Jesus and finally of Pentecost. All are interwoven with the line (which everyone says) from Lilian Moore: "When the wind blows, the quiet things speak." During the reading, the wind chimes might be taken down and passed from reader to reader, each blowing upon them before beginning the text.

To pass from the word to the oil, all sing a very short round (to any familiar tune):

> Wind in my hair!
> Breathe in the air!
> God's breeze is blowin'
> Through the sweet, soft oil!

OILS SHOWN, MIXED, BLESSED: First a portion of oil is taken from the bowl and placed in a small container with the words. "This is the oil of the olive, fruit of the tree of peace." Then the balsam, in this case a wax, is held up and called a "good smell of gentleness." All stand, extend their hands over the oil and balsam and repeat the words of blessing (taken in part from the rite for the consecration of the holy oils):

> Blessed art thou,
> Lord our God, King of the universe,
> for you have given us the oil of gladness.
> By the power of your holy breath,
> make this mixing of olive oil and balsam
> a sign and source of your blessing.

ANOINTING: Now a deacon (or the leader himself), wearing a stole, takes the small container of warm oil (warm from the wicks burning in the large bowl) and goes from person to person, signing each on the forehead and saying, "Put on the oil of gladness." A record of "Blowin' in the Wind" is played softly in the background and some people might wish to sing along.

CONCLUSION: All are asked to turn to the right, put their hands on the shoulders of the person now in front of them, and repeat loudly (let the voices move the air) this blessing (taken from the Pentecost service in the February 1973 *Liturgy*):

> The grace of Our Lord Jesus Christ,
> the love of God,
> and the Grand Slam of the Holy Spirit
> be with you
> and with your spirit. Amen.

All leave to the sound of blowing bagpipes.

Pentecost/Church Unity Octave

A liturgy during the Pentecost season or the Church Unity Octave (a celebration of hope) could include a simple ritual demonstrating the need for Christians to support and strengthen one another. Each participant receives a piece of string or a bright length of yarn, about a yard long. The leader asks one person to bring his or her string forward. The leader then breaks it in half and shows this to all the people, saying, "When one string is all alone it can be broken." He then asks for two volunteers to give him their strings. Twisting the two together he tries to break them, and if he does, he then announces, "When two strings are together they can be broken." This is repeated until the group of strings cannot be broken. He then says, "When four (or however many) strings are together they are too strong to break. The more strings you put together the stronger they are."

At this point he calls upon the assembled Christians to celebrate the strength of the church where *many* are one, by weaving (or tying) their strings all together in a long thick rope. A small group might be able to braid their pieces, a larger one will tend to wrap theirs together helter-skelter. As long as they are joined and the rope is strong, the ritual serves its purpose. This rope is then brought to the altar at the presentation of the gifts (if a eucharist is being celebrated), and wrapped around it or draped over it; if it is small, it may be used as a stole by the presider.

Welcome Summer

On June 21, summer begins. Welcome the sunrise with this American Indian song:

> Remember, remember the great life of the sun
> breathing on the earth
> it lies upon the earth
> to bring out life upon the earth
> life covering the earth.

Celebrate with a morning or evening fire to help the sun do its warming work. Bless the fire with this prayer (from the Roman Ritual):

> O Lord God, Father almighty,
> unfailing Ray and Source of all light,
> sanctify this new fire,
> and grant that after the darkness of this life
> we may come to thee who art light eternal.

Morning

Each summer morning face the rising sun in the east and pray together:

> O Lord, open my lips!
> And my mouth shall sing your praise!

And then part of Psalm 19 or another psalm:
> The heavens declare the glory of God,
>> the sky proclaims what he has made.
> Day speaks of it to day,
>> and night tells of it to night . . .

Or perhaps the ancient Druid prayer—"We seek and find in Thee the glory of the Dawn. We seek and find Thee when the darkness of the night has fled. The sleep of faith will ever lead from death to life . . . Inspire us with Thy holy will within the beauty of the morn, and send us forth to bless and purify all who would find Thee in the glory of the Dawn."

Then join hands and sing "Enter, Rejoice and Come In," or "Let the sun shine, let the sun shine in, the sun shine in . . . "

Evening

Each summer evening, face the setting sun in the west and pray together:
> Give thanks to the Lord for he is good!
> His love is everlasting.

And then part of Psalm 145 or another psalm:
> The Lord is merciful, tender of heart,
>> slow to anger, very loving,
>> and kind to everyone;
>> his tenderness embraces all his creatures . . .

Spend some quiet time talking and enjoying the cool of the evening and conclude with singing a song. Some good songs might be "Day is Done" ("And when you take my hand, my son . . . "), "Taps," "Praise God from whom all blessings flow . . . "

The Story of the Great Tree

In the beginning, a great black raven flew above the barren earth, carrying a single seed. He dropped it, and it fell on fertile soil where it grew into the first tree.

For centuries it grew and grew, until its top disappeared in the sky. The mountains creaked as the Great Tree shoved them aside, and the rivers changed courses to avoid it. Through all the four seasons it never stopped growing, and never lost one of its millions of leaves.

The Great Tree's roots bored down into the earth's center, into the cave of the Sleeping Dragon. The roots poked the dragon's belly and he woke with a roar, snapping and gnashing at the tree. For centuries he gnawed away at the roots until the Great Tree rumbled down, quaking the whole earth as it thundered down.

Many years later, earth's first people came by and saw the Great Tree helpless on its side. So beautiful and majestic was the tree that they wished it were alive. They hoisted the deadened tree trunk high, and sunk its root-end back into the fertile ground.

That summer the Great Tree sprung roots again and sprouted leaves. Even the raven returned, perched on one of the branches, and spoke to the first people:

"Your love has brought the Great Tree back to life. But it is gravely wounded and cannot live long. Because of your love, the Great Tree will bear a thousand different seeds as a gift for men and animals, so that the many trees can become your home. But the Great Tree will die, and there will never be another."

Autumn came and the Great Tree's leaves turned into the rainbow's every color. Pears and apples fell to the ground, and squirrels and chipmunks took them to every corner of the land. Eagles and egrets carried oranges and persimmons to other continents and the faraway islands. And the first people gathered walnuts, almonds, and hazlenuts to feed themselves during the coming winter.

That winter, the Great Tree did die, but the next spring saw woods and forests and jungles growing in every corner of the wide world. And in every new summer, trees grew the lushest and leaves the greenest on the longest day of the year when people sang songs, partied, and danced around their favorite trees.

A Summer Rain Dance

When there is a real need for rain, a group can gather outdoors, perhaps in the parched garden, and sit in a circle. The leader says:

OUR LAND IS THIRSTY, LORD!

Everyone takes up a handful of the dry earth, stands, and walks in a slow circle, tossing the dust slowly up toward the sky. All can sing, perhaps rather mournfully:
Oh, it ain't gonna rain no more, no more,
It ain't gonna rain no more.
How in the heck will I wash my neck,
If it ain't gonna rain no more!

Then the leader says:
LET US PRAY TO THE LORD OF THE SKIES AND CLOUDS TO SEND US RAIN!

Everyone finds a stick and joins in a circle dance, poking the sticks upwards to make holes in the heavens for the waters to come through. A spontaneous, wild chant is done with the dance. At the end, all gather together and sit down and someone tells the story of Elijah and the drought, with emphasis on the ending and its rain storm (see 1 Kings 17-18). At the conclusion, all take small containers of water and slowly pour the water on the plants and flowers and grass (and each other) and sing "Wade in the Water."

The Story of Guy Fawkes

Like all scarecrows, Guy Fawkes spent summer tied to a pole, dangling in the breeze, and scaring the birds away. He was not free. He gladly looked forward to the autumn bonfires which would free him to dance, blaze, and fly into the open sky.

But some people thought it was a waste of time to make new scarecrows every spring. Parliament passed a law: Scarecrows must guard the fields all year round!

Autumn came and no one took Guy down. The damp chill pierced his tattered clothing, and the rains soaked him to his strawbones.

"If I can't dance into the sky, Parliament will blow sky high!" swore Guy. And he wobbled off to London. He slipped into Parliament's cellars, and was about to ignite the barrels of gunpowder stored there, when he was caught.

Guy was quickly tried in court, found guilty, and sentenced to burn in the public square. They tossed him into a bonfire, and he crackled and popped. He caught ablaze, laughed aloud, and danced merrily upwards. He flew high and sang. He was free.

Some people were afraid other scarecrows might try the same. Parliament passed a new law: All scarecrows, without exception, were to be burned every November. When the scarecrows heard the new law, they grinned from ear to ear.

Morning Prayer in Autumn

Face east toward the rising sun. Fold your hands with the fingers extended. Raise the hands slowly above your head, then bow deeply, slowly, silently. Then, while bowing, say:
> Glory be to God.
> Glory be to Jesus.
> Glory be to the Holy Spirit.

Slowly straighten and lower your arms. If you wish, add to this a simple song of praise or a psalm. (Psalm 67 would be a good one, "May God have pity on us and bless us." It is short enough to memorize.)

Evening Prayer in Autumn

Sit quietly for awhile and watch the setting sun. Then stand, stretch your arms wide and raise them up high. Standing like this, find a way to say thanks for the day that has passed. Perhaps you can make up a way to sing one alleluia, or a group of alleluias. Some days it might be very long, other days very short. Some days loud, other days soft. Or you might use the word "shalom," the Hebrew word for peace. Then sit again and read aloud a psalm of thanks (23, 103, 104, 111, 131, 145, 146, 147 are good ones). Another prayer could be the Magnificat (Luke 1:46-55).

All the Saints

A month for thinking of the dead and celebrating our roots, the great and grand parents who got us here, the ancestors, the heroes and the saints. Make a list of all the people you know who have died this past year. Don't forget any animal friends. Display the family past in a tree going out and back as far as you can; get out old picture albums for long evenings. Let the celebrating-bright-dying leaves of autumn surround these. And talk about death, about what's to be . . .

    Oh, when the saints go marching in,
    Oh, when the saints go marching in,
    Oh Lord, I want to be in that number
    When the saints go marching in.

    2. Oh, when the new world is revealed . . .
    3. (Make up your own verses.)

Thanksgiving

Autumn comes near its end with the holiday called Thanksgiving. Here are three ideas for your family's Thanksgiving. Pick one out, make a plan for involving your family. Maybe it can be something that you will do every year on this festival.

1. Find a time when everyone is together. If you are going to someone else's home for dinner, the time might be while on the way. Each person gets a turn to say thank you to every other person for some one thing. "I'm thankful for Ann because of her laughter. And I'm thankful for Henry because he never stays angry with any of us . . . " Everyone should be given time to be thoughtful; that's all it takes to be thankful.

2. If your family is willing, plan together a Thanksgiving dinner that would be truly bountiful for most of the world (but not for us). Use rice and inexpensive vegetables, a little fruit, tea, and lots of imagination. But gather and eat in true gratitude to the Lord! Sing songs. Play games. Do crazy things! As a blessing for the meal read slowly Psalm 146: "Praise the Lord, O my soul."

3. If Thanksgiving is a day when you are together with grandparents and uncles and aunts and cousins, find a corner where you can draw people in and have them help you make a family tree. Get their help on your map of ancestors and relations. More than that, ask to hear the stories of when your parents were your age, stories of the grandparents' childhood, and even the stories their grandparents told them. Then you'll not only have your family tree, but you'll have some clues as to what kind of a tree it is!

Saint Nicholas and the Pawnbroker

The day before he became bishop, Nicholas pledged to give all his money to the poor. That night an angel came in a dream and said: "Nicholas, keep three sacks of gold under your bed!" Nicholas obeyed, but slept uncomfortably with the gold.

A year later the angel appeared again: "Nicholas! A poor merchant is selling his daughter into slavery to pay his debts. Toss a bag of gold into his chimney tonight!"

The girls was ransomed, but Nicholas still did not sleep well, with all his gold. Another year passed, and the angel appeared again: "Wake up, Nicholas! The merchant's daughter can't marry without a dowry. Toss a bag of gold through—" But before the angel could finish, Nicholas was already dashing out of the house.

A third year passed, and Nicholas could still not sleep well. The Angel returned. "Nicholas! The merchant will lose his pawnshop unless—" But before the angel finished, Nicholas was running down the dark streets of town.

The merchant kept his store and soon became prosperous. He stuffed the three empty moneybags, painted them golden, and hung them in front of his pawnshop. The three gold bags soon became the sign for all pawnshops, and Nicholas chuckled whenever he passed by them.

Now he could finally sleep well.

"How can I put my treasure in heaven? Give it to the poor."—St. Augustine

Song: "Guantanamera"
    With the poor people of the earth I will cast my lot.
    The streams of the mountain are more pleasing
        to me than the sea.

These ideas are largely the creations of Gabe Huck and Elizabeth McMahon Jeep. The stories were written by Robert Béla Wilhelm.

BE A NATURAL MAN

1. Samson, Samson, child of the sun, born to be wild and strong.

Samson, Samson, child of the sun, let your hair grow down long.

REFRAIN: Be a natural man, it's part of God's plan. Be a giant

Redwood tree! The strength you bear in the length of your

hair can set God's people free.

BE A NATURAL MAN

Samson, Samson, child of the sun,
Born to be wild and strong.
Samson, Samson, child of the sun,
Let your hair grow down long.

Be a natural man,
It's part of God's plan.
Be a giant Redwood tree!
The strength you bear
In the length of your hair
Can set God's people free.

Samson, Samson, child of the sun,
Delilah sets a trap in her lair.
Samson, Samson, she might be fun,
But she's out to get your hair.

Refrain:

Samson, Samson, look what you have done,
They have made you a fool and a slave.
Samson, Samson, child of the sun,
Who can you hope to save?

Refrain:

Samson, Samson, child of the sun,
Your plight looks rather dim,
Samson, Samson, child of the sun,
Let your hair grow long again!

Refrain:

WOMEN OF ISRAEL DANCE!

REFRAIN: Women of Is-ra-el dance; Women of Is-ra-el weep;

Women of Is-ra-el laugh, and the earth will move under your

feet! La la la la la la la; La la la la la la la.

(SMALL NOTES FOR HARMONY)

1. Sing the song of Sarah; From her God's people began.

Sing the song of Deborah; Her wisdom brought peace to the

land. La la la la la la la; La la la la la la la. -REFRAIN:

WOMEN OF ISRAEL DANCE!

Refrain:
Women of Israel dance;
Women of Israel weep;
Women of Israel laugh,
And the earth will move under your feet!
La la la la la la la,
La la la la la la la.

Sing the song of Sarah;
From her God's people began.
Sing the song of Deborah;
Her wisdom brought peace to the land.
La la la la la la la,
La la la la la la la. Refrain:

Sing the song of Esther,
Sing of faithful Ruth.
Sing the song of Rachel;
Women of courage and truth.
La la la la la la la,
La la la la la la la. Refrain:

Sing the song of Nazareth;
Joy for a sorrowful world.
Sing the song of freedom
From the heart of a very young girl.
La la la la la la la,
La la la la la la la. Refrain:

Notes: This song will be enhanced by retelling the
stories of Sarah (Gen 17:15ff; 21:1-12)
Rachel (Gen 29-31)
Deborah (Judges 4-5)
The Book of Ruth
The Book of Esther
Mary (Lk 1:26-45)

Try a circle dance with this tune, changing
directions with each phrase of the Refrain.

144

THE GOOD THINGS

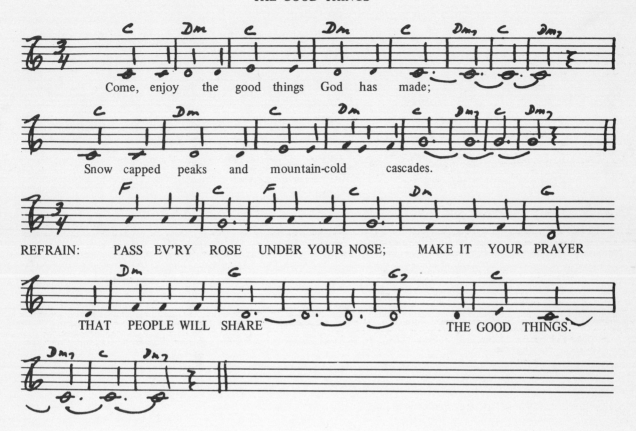

Come, enjoy the good things God has made;

Snow capped peaks and mountain-cold cascades.

REFRAIN: PASS EV'RY ROSE UNDER YOUR NOSE; MAKE IT YOUR PRAYER

THAT PEOPLE WILL SHARE THE GOOD THINGS.

THE GOOD THINGS

Come, enjoy the good things God has made;
Snow capped peaks and mountain-cold cascades.

Refrain: Pass ev'ry rose
                 Under your nose!
             Make it your prayer
                 That people will share
             The Good Things.

Come, enjoy the good things God has made;
Peanut butter toast with marmalade.

Refrain:

Come, enjoy the good things God has made;
A box of shells and secret things to trade.

Refrain:

Come, enjoy the good things God has made;
Handsome clothes that will not shrink or fade.

Refrain:

Come, enjoy the good things God has made;
Choc'late cake with ice-cold lemonade.

Refrain:

Note: Invite the children to add their own verses.

PEACEABLE PEOPLE

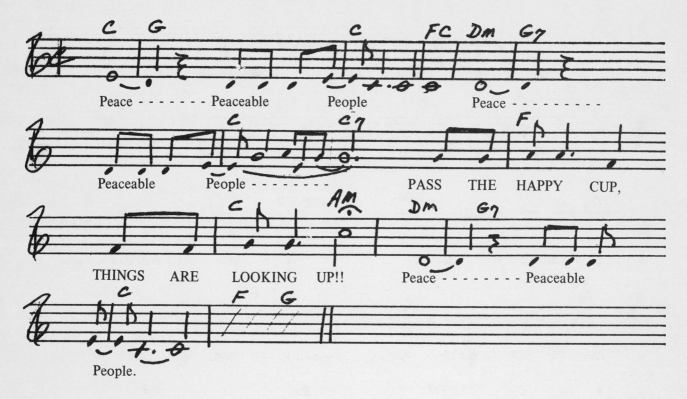

Peace - - - - - - - Peaceable People Peace - - - - - - - -
Peaceable People - - - - - - - - PASS THE HAPPY CUP,
THINGS ARE LOOKING UP!! Peace - - - - - - - Peaceable
People.

(As the song builds raise the key to *D* and finally to *E*.)

PEACEABLE PEOPLE

Peace - - - - - - - Peaceable People
Peace - - - - - - - Peaceable People
Pass the happy cup,
Things are looking up!
Peace - - - - - - - Peaceable People

(You may add other words in the place of *People*;
e.g., table, brothers, sisters, mothers, fathers,
oceans, mountains, valleys, canyons, Kingdom.)

146

LET ALL THE EARTH SING HIS PRAISE
(The Elephant Song)

Tom Parker

LET ALL THE EARTH SING HIS PRAISE — AND

JOY-FUL VOICES RAISE, FOR 'HIS MER-CY REACHES

OUT TO EV'RY LAND.   1. SING MEN OF DISTANT CHINA,

TELL OF HIS WORTH FROM IT-A-LY TO THE IC-Y SEA OF THE

NORTH;   MEN WHO RIDE EL-E-PHANTS AND MEN WHO WORK IN

STORES: JE-SUS IS LORD OF ALL THE EARTH   LET ALL THE

ADDITIONAL VERSES

2. Come Dance and run before him, all you who can
From Baltimore to the distant shore of Japan
Men who plow the endless plains, your saviour is at hand:
Jesus—the hope of ev'ry land!

3. Hear us men of France and Sweden, boys of Peru,
all children of the sea, girls of Brittany too—
Babies who ride on camels trudging seas of sand,
Jesus your brother's calling you!

4. Sing men from Manitoba, Kenya and Zaire
The South Sea Islands and Scottish highlands so fair;
Men who cut sugar cane and build their homes of straw—
Jesus is living everywhere!

5. Sing sages of the East and give him your best
from Bleecker Street to the fields of Wheat in the West!
Come tired and hungry men who long to live in peace—
Jesus your shepherd brings you rest!

[Note: verse 4 was changed as there is no longer any such place as the Congo.]

147

AN ALL PURPOSE PSALM-SONG

Refrain Melody: traditional   Words: Ps 103
Verse Melody: Tom Parker   Paraphrased by Tom Parker

The old "Eightfold Alleluia" melody, used here as a refrain, can be sung with almost any words: "Alleluia 8x"
or "Jesus is Lord," or longer patterns: "Jesus Loves us, Jesus Saves us, He will heal us and forgive us," etc.
This song can be learned rapidly if the cantor sings the verses, but children can sing the verses with more practice.

APPENDIXES

DIRECTORY FOR MASSES WITH CHILDREN

INTRODUCTION

1. The Church shows special concern for baptized children who have yet to be fully initiated through the sacraments of confirmation and eucharist as well as for children who have only recently been admitted to holy communion. Today the circumstances in which children grow up are not favorable to their spiritual progress.[1] In addition, sometimes parents barely fulfill the obligations of Christian education which they undertake at the baptism of their children.

2. In bringing up children in the Church a special difficulty arises from the fact that liturgical celebrations, especially the eucharist, cannot fully exercise their innate pedagogical force upon children.[2] Although the mother tongue may now be used at Mass, still the words and signs have not been sufficiently adapted to the capacity of children.

In fact, even in daily life children cannot always understand everything that they experience with adults, and they easily become weary. It cannot be expected, moreover, that everything in the liturgy will always be intelligible to them. Nonetheless, we may fear spiritual harm if over the years children repeatedly experience in the Church things that are scarcely comprehensible to them: recent psychological study has established how profoundly children are formed by the religious experience of infancy and early childhood, according to their individual religious capacity.[3]

3. The Church follows its Master, who "put his arms around the children . . . and blessed them" (Mark 10: 16). It cannot leave children to themselves. The Second Vatican Council had spoken in the Constitution on the Liturgy about the need of liturgical adaptation for various groups.[4] Soon afterwards, especially in the first Synod of Bishops held in Rome in 1967, the Church began to consider how participation of children could be made easier. On the occasion of the Synod the president of the Consilium for the Implementation of the Constitution on the Liturgy said explicitly that it could not be a matter of "creating some entirely special rite but rather of retaining, shortening, or omitting some elements or of making a better selection of texts."[5]

4. All the details of eucharistic celebration with a congregation were determined in the General Instruction of the revised *Roman Missal*, published in 1969. Then this congregation began to prepare a special directory for Masses with children, as a supplement to the instruction. This was done in response to repeated petitions from the entire Catholic world and with the cooperation of men and women specialists from almost every nation.

5. Like the General Instruction, this directory reserves some adaptations to conferences of bishops or individual bishops.[6]

With regard to adaptations of the Mass which may be necessary for children in a given country but which cannot be included in this general directory, the conferences of bishops should submit proposals to the Apostolic See, in accord with article 40 of the Constitution on the Liturgy. These adaptations are to be introduced only with the consent of the Apostolic See.

6. The directory is concerned with children who have not yet entered the period of pre-adolescence. It does not speak directly of children who are physically or mentally retarded because a broader adaptation is sometimes necessary for them.[7] Nevertheless, the following norms may also be applied to the retarded, with the necessary changes.

7. The first chapter of the directory (nos. 8-15) gives a kind of foundation by considering the different ways in which children are introduced to the eucharistic liturgy. The second chapter briefly treats Masses with adults, in which children also take part (nos. 16-19). Finally, the third chapter (nos. 20-54) treats at greater length Masses with children, in which only some adults take part.

CHAPTER I: The Introduction of Children to the Eucharistic Celebration

8. A fully Christian life cannot be conceived without participation in the liturgical services in which the faithful, gathered into a single assembly, celebrate the paschal mystery. Therefore, the religious initiation of children must be in harmony with this purpose.[8] By baptizing infants, the church expresses its confidence in the gifts received from this sacrament; thus it must be concerned that the baptized grow in communion with Christ and the brethren. Sharing in the eucharist is the sign and pledge of this very communion. Children are prepared for eucharistic communion and introduced more deeply into its meaning. It is not right to separate such liturgical and eucharistic formation from the general human and Christian education of children. Indeed it would be harmful if liturgical formation lacked such a foundation.

9. For this reason all who have a part in the formation of children should consult and work together. In this way even if children already have some feeling for God and the things of God, they may also experience the human values which are found in the eucharistic celebration, depending upon their age and personal progress. These values are the activity of the community, exchange of greetings, capacity to listen and to seek and grant pardon, expression of gratitude, experience of symbolic actions, a meal of friendship, and festive celebration.[9]

Eucharistic catechesis, which is mentioned in no. 12, should go beyond such human values. Thus, depending on their age, psychological condition, and social situation, children may gradually open their minds to the perception of Christian values and the celebration of the mystery of Christ.[10]

10. The Christian family has the greatest role in teaching these Christian and human values.[11] Thus Christian education, provided by parents and other educators, should be strongly encouraged in relation to liturgical formation of children as well.

By reason of the responsibility freely accepted at the baptism of their children, parents are bound in conscience to teach them gradually to pray. This they do by praying with them each day and by introducing them to prayers said privately.[12] If children are prepared in this way, even from their early years, and do take part in the Mass with their family when they wish, they will easily begin to sing and to pray in the liturgical community, indeed they will have some kind of foretaste of the eucharistic mystery.

If the parents are weak in faith but still wish their children to receive Christian formation, at least they should be urged to share the human values mentioned above with their children. On occasion, they should be encouraged to participate in meetings of parents and in non-eucharistic celebrations with their children.

11. The Christian communities to which the individual families belong or in which the children live also have a responsibility toward children baptized in the Church. By giving witness to the gospel, living fraternal charity, actively celebrating the mysteries of Christ, the Christian community is the best school of Christian and liturgical formation for the children who live in it.

Within the Christian community, godparents and others with special concern who are moved by apostolic zeal can help greatly in the necessary catechesis of children of families which are unable to fulfill their own responsibility in Christian education.

In particular these ends can be served by preschool programs, Catholic schools, and various kinds of classes for children.

12. Even in the case of children, the liturgy itself always exerts its own proper didactic force.[13] Yet within programs of catechetical, scholastic, and parochial formation, the necessary importance should be given to catechesis on the Mass.[14] This catechesis should be directed to the child's active, conscious, and authentic participation.[15] "Clearly accommodated to the age and mentality of the children, it should attempt, through the principal rites and prayers, to convey the meaning of the Mass, including a participation in the whole life of the Church."[16] This is especially true of the text of the eucharistic prayer and of the acclamations with which the children take part in this prayer.

Special mention should be made of the catechesis through which children are prepared for first communion. Not only should they learn the truths of faith concerning the eucharist, but they should also understand how from first communion on—prepared by penance according to their need and fully initiated into the body of Christ—they may actively participate in the eucharist with the people of God and have their place at the Lord's table and in the community of the brethren.

13. Various kinds of celebrations may also play a major role in the liturgical formation of children and in their preparation for the Church's liturgical life. By the very fact of celebration children easily come to appreciate some liturgical elements, for example, greetings, silence, and common praise (especially when this is sung in common). Such celebrations, however, should avoid having too didactic a character.

14. Depending on the capacity of the children, the word of God should have a greater and greater place in these celebrations. In fact, as the spiritual capacity of children develops, celebrations of the word of God in the strict sense should be held frequently, especially during Advent and Lent.[17] These will help greatly to develop in the children an appreciation of the word of God.

15. Over and above what has been said already, all liturgical and eucharistic formation should be directed toward a greater and greater response to the Gospel in the daily life of the children.

CHAPTER II: Masses with Adults in Which Children Also Participate

16. Parish Masses are celebrated in many places, especially on Sundays and holydays, with a large number of adults and a smaller number of children. On such occasions the witness of adult believers can have a great effect upon the children. Adults can also benefit spiritually from experiencing the part which the children have within the Christian community. If children take part in these Masses together with their parents and other members of their family, this should be of great help to the Christian spirit of families.

Infants who as yet are unable or unwilling to take part in the Mass may be brought in at the end of Mass to be blessed together with the rest of the community. This may be done, for example, if parish helpers have been taking care of them in a separate area.

17. Nevertheless, in Masses of this kind it is necessary to take great care that the children do not feel neglected because of their inability to participate or to understand what happens and what is proclaimed in the celebration. Some account should be taken of their presence, for example, by speaking to them directly in the introductory comments (as at the beginning and the end of Mass) and in part of the homily.

Sometimes, moreover, it will perhaps be appropriate, if the physical arrangements and the circumstances of the community permit, to celebrate the liturgy of the word, including a homily, with the children in a separate area that is not too far removed. Then, before the eucharistic liturgy begins, the children are led to the place where the adults have meanwhile been celebrating their own liturgy of the word.

18. It may also be very helpful to give some tasks to the children. They may, for example, bring forward the gifts or sing one or other of the parts of Mass.

19. Sometimes, if the number of children is large, it may be suitable to plan the Masses so that they correspond better to the needs of the children. In this case the homily should be directed to the children but in such a way that adults may also benefit from it. In addition to the adaptations now in the Order of Mass, one or other of the special adaptations described below may be employed in a Mass celebrated with adults in which children also participate, where the bishop permits such adaptations.

CHAPTER III: Masses with Children in Which Only a Few Adults Participate

20. In addition to the Masses in which children take part with their parents and other members of their family (which are not always possible everywhere), Masses with children in which only some adults take part are recommended, especially during the week. From the beginning of the liturgical restoration it has been clear to everyone that some adaptations are necessary in these Masses.[18]

Such adaptations, but only those of a more general kind, will be considered below (nos. 38-54).

21. It is always necessary to keep in mind that through these eucharistic celebrations children must be led toward the celebration of Mass with adults, especially the Masses in which the Christian community comes together on Sundays.[19] Thus, apart from adaptations which are necessary because of the children's age, the result should not be entirely special rites which differ too greatly from the Order of Mass celebrated with a congregation.[20] The purpose of the various elements should always correspond with what is said in the General Instruction of the *Roman Missal* on individual points, even if at times for pastoral reasons an absolute *identity* cannot be insisted upon.

OFFICES AND MINISTRIES IN THE CELEBRATION

22. The principles of active and conscious participation are in a sense even more valid for Masses celebrated with children. Every effort should be made to increase this participation and to make it more intense. For this reason as many children as possible should have special parts in the celebration, for example: preparing the place and the altar (see no. 29), acting as cantor (see no. 24), singing in a choir, playing musical instruments (see no. 32), proclaiming the readings (see nos. 24 and 47), responding during the homily (see no. 48), reciting the intentions of the general intercessions, bringing the gifts to the altar, and performing similar activities in accord with the usage of various communities (see no. 34).

To encourage participation it will sometimes be helpful to have several additions, for example, the insertion of motives for giving thanks before the priest begins the dialogue of the preface.

In all this one should keep in mind that external activities will be fruitless and even harmful if they do not serve the internal participation of the children. Thus religious silence has its importance even in Masses with children (see no. 37). The children should not be allowed to forget that all the forms of participation reach their high point in eucharistic communion when the body and blood of Christ are received as spiritual nourishment.[21]

23. It is the responsibility of the priest who celebrates with children to make the celebration festive, fraternal, meditative.[22] Even more than in Masses with adults, the priest should try to bring about this kind of spirit. It will depend upon his personal preparation and his manner of acting and speaking with others.

Above all, the priest should be concerned about the dignity, clarity, and simplicity of his actions and gestures. In speaking to the children he should express himself so that he will be easily understood, while avoiding any childish style of speech.

The free use of introductory comments[23] will lead children to a genuine liturgical participation, but these explanations should not be merely didactic.

It will help in reaching the hearts of the children if the priest sometimes uses his own words when he gives invitations, for example, at the penitential rite, the prayer over the gifts, the Lord's Prayer, the sign of peace, and communion.

24. Since the eucharist is always the action of the entire Church community, the participation of at least some adults is desirable. These should be present not as monitors but as participants, praying with the children and helping them to the extent necessary.

With the consent of the pastor or the rector of the church, one of the adults may speak to the children after the gospel, especially if the priest finds it difficult to adapt himself to the mentality of the children. In this matter the norms of the Congregation for the Clergy should be observed.

The diversity of ministries should also be encouraged in Masses with children so that the Mass may be evidently the celebration of a community.[24] For example, readers and cantors, whether children or adults, should be employed. In this way variety will keep the children from becoming tired because of the sameness of voices.

PLACE AND TIME OF CELEBRATION

25. The primary place for the eucharistic celebration for children is the church. Within the church, however, a space should be carefully chosen, if available, which will be suited to the number of participants. It should be a place where the children can conduct themselves freely according to the demands of a living liturgy that is suited to their age.

If the church does not satisfy these demands, it will sometimes be suitable to celebrate the eucharist with children outside a sacred place. Then the place chosen should be appropriate and worthy.[25]

26. The time of day chosen for Masses with children should correspond with the circumstances of their lives so that they may be most open to hearing the word of God and to celebrating the eucharist.

27. Weekday Mass in which children participate can certainly be celebrated with greater effect and less danger of weariness if it does not take place every day (for example, in boarding schools). Moreover, preparation can be more careful if there is a longer interval between celebrations.

Sometimes it is preferable to have common prayer to which the children may contribute spontaneously, either a common meditation or a celebration of the word of God. These celebrations continue the eucharist and lead to deeper participation in later eucharistic celebrations.

28. When the number of children who celebrate the eucharist together is very great, attentive and conscious participation becomes more difficult. Therefore, if possible, several groups should be formed; these should not be set up rigidly according to age but with regard to the progress of religious formation and catechetical preparation of the children.

During the week such groups may be invited to the sacrifice of the Mass on different days.

PREPARATION FOR THE CELEBRATION

29. Each eucharistic celebration with children should be carefully prepared beforehand, especially with regard to prayers, songs, readings, and intentions of the general intercessions. This should be done in discussion with the adults and with the children who will have a special ministry in these Masses. If possible, some of the children should take part in preparing and ornamenting the place of celebration and preparing the chalice with the paten and cruets. Over and above the appropriate internal participation, such activity will help to develop the spirit of community celebration.

SINGING AND MUSIC

30. Singing is of great importance in all celebrations, but it is to be especially encouraged in every way for Masses celebrated with children, in view of their special affinity for music.[26] The culture of various groups and the capabilities of the children present should be taken into account.

If possible the acclamations should be sung by the children rather than recited, especially the acclamations which are a part of the eucharistic prayer.

31. To facilitate the children's participation in singing the Gloria, profession of faith, Sanctus, and Agnus Dei, it is permissible to use music set to appropriate vernacular texts, accepted by the competent authority, even if these do not agree completely with the liturgical texts.[27]

32. The use of "musical instruments may be of great help" in Masses with children, especially if they are played by the children themselves.[28] The playing of instruments will help to support the singing or to encourage the reflection of the children; sometimes by themselves instruments express festive joy and the praise of God.

Care should always be taken, however, that the music does not prevail over the singing or become a distraction rather than a help to the children. Music should correspond to the purpose which is attached to the different periods for which it is introduced into the Mass.

With these precautions and with special and necessary concern, music that is technically produced may be also used in Masses with children, in accord with norms established by the conferences of bishops.

GESTURES AND ACTIONS

33. The development of gestures, postures, and actions is very important for Masses with children in view of the nature of the liturgy as an activity of the entire man and in view of the psychology of children. This should be done in harmony with the age and local usage. Much depends not only on the actions of the priest,[29] but also on the manner in which the children conduct themselves as a community.

If a conference of bishops, in accord with the norm of the General Instruction of the *Roman Missal* [30] adapts the actions of the Mass to the mentality of the people, it should give consideration to the special condition of children or should determine such adaptations for children only.

34. Among the actions which are considered under this heading, processions deserve special mention as do other activities which involve physical participation.

The processional entrance of the children with the priest may help them to experience a sense of the communion that is thus constituted.[31] The participation of at least some children in the procession with the book of gospels makes clear the presence of Christ who announces his word to the people. The procession of children with the chalice and the gifts expresses clearly the value and meaning of the preparation of gifts. The communion procession, if properly arranged, helps greatly to develop the piety of the children.

VISUAL ELEMENTS

35. The liturgy of the Mass contains many visual elements, and these should be given great prominence with children. This is especially true of the particular visual elements in the course of the liturgical year, for example, the veneration of the cross, the Easter candle, the lights on the feast of the Presentation of the Lord, and the variety of colors and liturgical ornaments.

In addition to the visual elements that belong to the celebration and to the place of celebration, it is appropriate to introduce other elements which will permit children to perceive visually the great deeds of God in creation and redemption and thus support their prayer. The liturgy should never appear as something dry and merely intellectual.

36. For the same reason the use of pictures prepared by the children themselves may be useful, for example, to illustrate a homily, to give a visual dimension to the intentions of the general intercessions, or to inspire reflection.

SILENCE

37. Even in Masses with children "silence should be observed at the proper time as a part of the celebration"[32] lest too great a role be given to external action. In their own way children are genuinely capable of reflection. They need, however, a kind of introduction so that they will learn how to reflect within themselves, meditate briefly, or praise God and pray to him in their hearts[33] for example after the homily or after communion.[34]

Besides this, with even greater care than in Masses with adults, the liturgical texts should be spoken intelligibly and unhurriedly, with the necessary pauses.

THE PARTS OF MASS

38. The general structure of the Mass, which "in some sense consists of two parts, namely, the liturgy of the word and the liturgy of the eucharist," should always be maintained as should some rites to open and conclude the celebration.[35] Within individual parts of the celebration the adaptations which follow seem necessary if children are truly to experience, in their own way and according to the psychological patterns of childhood, "the mystery of faith . . . by means of rites and prayers."[36]

39. Some rites and texts should never be adapted for children lest the difference between Masses with children and the Masses with adults become too great.[37] These are "the acclamations and the responses of the faithful to the greetings of the priest,"[38] the Lord's Prayer, and the trinitarian formula at the end of the blessing with which the priest concludes the Mass. It is urged, moreover, that children should become accustomed to the Nicene Creed little by little, while the use of the Apostles' Creed mentioned in no. 49 is permitted.

a) Introductory Rite

40.   The introductory rite of Mass has the purpose "that the faithful, assembling in unity, should constitute a communion and should prepare themselves properly for hearing the word of God and celebrating the eucharist worthily."[39] Therefore every effort should be made to create this disposition in the children and to avoid any excess of rites in this part of Mass.

It is sometimes proper to omit one or other element of the introductory rite or perhaps to enlarge one of the elements. There should always be at least some introductory element, which is completed by the opening prayer or collect. In choosing individual elements one should be careful that each one be used at times and that none be entirely neglected.

b) Reading and Explanation of the Word of God

41.   Since readings taken from holy scripture constitute "the principal part of the liturgy of the word,"[40] biblical reading should never be omitted even in Masses celebrated with children.

42.   With regard to the number of readings on Sundays and feast days, the decrees of the conferences of bishops should be observed. If three or even two readings on Sundays or weekdays can be understood by children only with difficulty, it is permissible to read two or only one of them, but the reading of the gospel should never be omitted.

43.   If all the readings assigned to the day seem to be unsuited to the capacity of the children, it is permissible to choose readings or a reading either from the *Lectionary for Mass* or directly from the Bible, taking into account the liturgical seasons. It is urged, moreover, that the individual conferences of bishops prepare lectionaries for Masses with children.

If because of the limited capabilities of the children it seems necessary to omit one or other verse of a biblical reading, this should be done cautiously and in such a way "that the meaning of the texts or the sense and, as it were, style of the scriptures are not mutilated."[41]

44.   In the choice of readings the criterion to be followed is the quality rather than the quantity of the texts from the scriptures. In itself a shorter reading is not always more suited to children than a lengthy reading. Everything depends upon the spiritual advantage which the reading can offer to children.

45.   In the biblical texts "God speaks to his people . . . and Christ himself is present through his word in the assembly of the faithful."[42] Paraphrases of scripture should therefore be avoided. On the other hand, the uses of translations which may already exist for the catechesis of children and which are accepted by the competent authority is recommended.

46.   Verses of psalms, carefully selected in accord with the understanding of children, or singing in the form of psalmody or the alleluia with a simple verse should be sung between the readings. The children should always have a part in this singing, but sometimes a reflective silence may be substituted for the singing.

If only a single reading is chosen, there may be singing after the homily.

47.   All the elements which will help to understand the readings should be given great consideration so that the children may make the biblical readings their own and may come more and more to appreciate the value of God's word.

Among these elements are the introductory comments which may precede the readings[43] and help the children to listen better and more fruitfully, either by explaining the context or by introducing the text itself. In interpreting and illustrating the readings from the scriptures in the Mass on a saint's day, an account of the life of the saint may be given not only in the homily but even before the readings in the form of a commentary.

Where the text of the readings suggest, it may be helpful to have the children read it with parts distributed among them, as is provided for the reading of the Lord's Passion during Holy Week.

48.   The homily in which the word of God is unfolded should be given great prominence in all Masses with children. Sometimes the homily intended for children should become a dialogue with them, unless it is preferred that they should listen in silence.

49.   If the profession of faith occurs at the end of the liturgy of the word, the Apostles' Creed may be used with children, especially because it is part of their catechetical formation.

c) Presidential Prayers

50.   The priest is permitted to choose from the *Roman Missal* texts of presidential prayers more suited to children, keeping in mind the liturgical season, so that he may truly associate the children with himself.

51.   Sometimes this principle of selection is insufficient if the children are to consider the prayers as the expression of their own lives and their own religious experience, since the prayers were composed for adult Christians.[44] In this case the text of prayers of the *Roman Missal* may be adapted to the needs of children, but this should be done in such a way that, preserving

the purpose of the prayer and to some extent its substance as well, the priest avoids anything that is foreign to the literary genre of a presidential prayer, such as moral exhortations or a childish manner of speech.

52. The eucharistic prayer is of the greatest importance in the eucharist celebrated with children because it is the high point of the entire celebration.[45] Much depends upon the manner in which the priest proclaims this prayer[46] and in which the children take part by listening and making their acclamations.

The disposition of mind required for this central part of the celebration, the calm and reverence with which everything is done, should make the children as attentive as possible. They should be attentive to the real presence of Christ on the altar under the species of bread and wine, to his offering, to the thanksgiving through him and with him and in him, and to the offering of the Church which is made during the prayer and by which the faithful offer themselves and their lives with Christ to the eternal Father in the Holy Spirit.

For the present, the four eucharistic prayers approved by the supreme authority for Masses with adults are to be employed and kept in liturgical use until the Apostolic See makes other provision for Masses with children.

d) *Rites before Communion*

53. At the end of the eucharistic prayer, the Lord's Prayer, the breaking of bread, and the invitation to communion should always follow.[47] These elements have the principal significance in the structure of this part of the Mass.

e) *Communion and the Following Rites*

54. Everything should be done so that the children who are properly disposed and who have already been admitted to the eucharist may go to the holy table calmly and with recollection, so that they may take part fully in the eucharistic mystery. If possible there should be singing, accommodated to the understanding of children, during the communion procession.[48]

The invitation which precedes the final blessing[49] is important in Masses with children. Before they are dismissed they need some repetition and application of what they heard, but this should be done in a very few words. In particular, this is the appropriate time to express the connection between the liturgy and life.

At least sometimes, depending on the liturgical seasons and the different circumstances in the life of the children, the priest should use the richer forms of blessing, but he should always retain the trinitarian formula with the sign of the cross at the end.[50]

55. The contents of the directory are intended to help children quickly and joyfully to encounter Christ together in the eucharistic celebration and to stand in the presence of the Father with him.[51] If they are formed by conscious and active participation in the eucharistic sacrifice and meal, they should learn day by day, at home and away from home, to proclaim Christ to others among their family and among their peers, by living the "faith, which expresses itself through love" (Galatians 5:6).

This directory was prepared by the Congregation for Divine Worship. On October 22, 1973, the Supreme Pontiff, Paul VI, approved and confirmed it and ordered that it be made public.

From the office of the Congregation for Divine Worship, November 1, 1973, the solemnity of All Saints.

By special mandate of the Supreme Pontiff.

Jean Card. Villot
Secretary of State
+H. Bugnini
  Titular Archbishop of Diocletiana
  Secretary of the Congregation for Divine Worship

NOTES

1. See Congregation for the Clergy, *Directorium Catechisticum Generale* [=DCG], no. 5: *AAS*, 64 (1972) 101-102.
2. See Vatican Council II, Constitution on the Liturgy, *Sacrosanctum Concilium* [=L], no. 33.
3. See DCG 78: *AAS*, 64 (1972) 146-147.
4. See L 38; also Congregation for Divine Worship, instruction *Actio pastoralis*, May 15, 1969: *AAS*, 61 (1969) 806-811.
5. First Synod of Bishops, Liturgy: *Notitiae*, 3 (1967) 368.
6. See below, nos. 19, 32, 33.
7. See Order of Mass with children who are deafmutes for German-speaking countries, confirmed June 26, 1970, by this congregation (prot. no. 1546/70).
8. See L 14, 19.
9. See DCG 25: *AAS*, 64 (1972) 114.
10. See Vatican Council II, Declaration on Christian Education, *Gravissimum educationis*, no. 2.
11. See *Ibid.*, 3.
12. See DCG 78: *AAS*, 64 (1972) 147.
13. See L 33.
14. See Congregation of Rites, instruction *Eucharisticum mysterium* [=EM], May 25, 1967, no. 14: *AAS*, 59 (1967) 550.

155

15. See DCG 25: *AAS*, 64 (1972) 114.
16. See EM 14: *AAS*, 59 (1967) 550; also DCG 57: *AAS*, 64 (1972) 131.
17. See L 35, 4.
18. See above, no. 3.
19. See L 42, 106.
20. See first Synod of Bishops, Liturgy: *Notitiae*, 3 (1967) 368.
21. See General Instruction of the Roman Missal [=IG], no. 56.
22. See below, no. 37.
23. See IG 11.
24. See L 28.
25. See IG 253.
26. See IG 19.
27. See Congregation of Rites, instruction *Musicam sacram*, March 5, 1967, no. 55: *AAS*, 59 (1967) 316.
28. *Ibid.*, 62: *AAS*, 59 (1967) 318.
29. See above, no. 23.
30. See IG 21.
31. See IG 24.
32. See IG 23.
33. See instruction *Eucharisticum mysterium*, no. 38: *AAS*, 59 (1967) 562.
34. See IG 23.
35. See IG 8.
36. See L 48.
37. See above, no. 21.
38. IG 15.
39. IG 24.
40. IG 38.
41. See *Lectionary for Mass*, introduction, no. 7d.
42. IG 33.
43. See IG 11.
44. See Consilium for the Implementation of the Constitution on the Liturgy, Instruction on Translation of Liturgical Texts, January 25, 1969, no. 20: *Notitiae*, 5 (1969) 7.
45. See IG 54.
46. See above, nos. 23, 37.
47. See above, no. 23.
48. See instruction *Musicam sacram*, no. 32: *AAS*, 59 (1967) 309.
49. See IG 11.
50. See above, no. 39.
51. See Eucharistic Prayer II.

BIBLIOGRAPHY

1. GENERAL INTRODUCTION

Aries, Philippe. *Centuries of Childhood: A Social History of Family Life.* Trans. Robert Baldick. New York: Alfred A. Knopf, 1962.

Canadian Conference of Catholic Bishops. National Bulletin on Liturgy 11 (March–April 1978).

Clanton, Bruce. "Jesus, the Child in God." *Liturgy* 24 (July–August 1979) 33–34.

Cooke, Bernard. "Living Liturgy: Life as Liturgy." In *Emerging Issues in Religious Education.* Gloria Durka and Joanmarie Smith, eds. New York: Paulist Press, 1976. 116–127.

Donaldson, Margaret. *Children's Minds.* New York: W. W. Norton and Co., 1978.

Hovda, Robert. *Strong, Loving and Wise.* Washington: The Liturgical Conference, 1976.

Hovda, Robert, and Huck, Gabe. *There's No Place Like People.* Washington: The Liturgical Conference, 1969.

Huck, Gabe. *Liturgy Needs Community Needs Liturgy.* New York: Paulist Press, 1973.

Huck, Gabe, and Sloyan, Virginia. *Parishes and Families: A Model for Christian Formation Through Liturgy.* Washington: The Liturgical Conference, 1973.

Lutheran Book of Worship. Minneapolis: Augsburg, 1978.

Manual on the Liturgy: Lutheran Book of Worship. Minneapolis: Augsburg, 1978.

Mitchell, Nathan. "The Once and Future Child: Towards a Theology of Childhood." *The Living Light* 12 (Fall 1975) 423–437.

Neville, Gwen K., and Westerhoff, John H. III. *Learning Through Liturgy.* New York: Seabury Press, 1978.

Pieper, Joseph. *In Tune with the World: A Theory of Festivity.* Chicago: Franciscan Herald Press, 1978.

Rabalais, Maria, and Hall, Howard. *Children Celebrate.* New York: Paulist Press, 1974.

Rahner, Karl. "Ideas for a Theology of Childhood." *Theological Investigations* 8:33–50.

Reeder, Rachel, ed. *Liturgy: Celebrating with Children.* vol. 1, no. 3. Washington: The Liturgical Conference, 1981.

Rochelle, J. C. *Create and Celebrate.* Philadelphia: Fortress Press, 1971.

Schmidt, Gail Ramshaw. "To Fear and Love God: Children and the Liturgy." *Liturgy* 24 (July–August 1979) 21–24.

Sloyan, Virginia, ed. *Liturgy Committee Handbook.* Washington: The Liturgical Conference, 1971.

Sokol, Frank C. "Turning Pumpkins into Coaches: Liturgy with Children." In *Christian Initiation Resources,* vol. 2, no. 1. James B. Dunning and William J. Reedy, eds. New York: Sadlier Press, 1981.

2. PRAYER

Carroll, James. *Wonder and Worship.* Paramus, N.J.: Newman Press, 1970.

Curran, Dolores. *Family Prayer.* West Mystic, Conn.: Twenty-Third Publications, 1979.

Huck, Gabe. *A Book of Family Prayer.* New York: Seabury Press, 1979.

Klug, Ron, and Klug, Lyn. *Family Prayers.* Minneapolis: Augsburg, 1979.

Pfeifer, Carl, and Manternach, Janaan. *Living Waters: Prayers of Our Heritage.* New York: Paulist Press, 1978.

Prayers for the Domestic Church: A Handbook for Worship in the Home. Easton, Kans.: Shantivanum House of Prayer, 1979.

Schroeder, Ted and Linda, et al., *Celebrate While We Wait: Family Devotional Resources for Advent and Christmas Too.* St. Louis: Concordia, 1977.

Sokol, Frank C. "The Rites of Young Christians." In *Liturgy: The Rites of Gathering and Sending Forth,* vol. 1, no. 4. Rachel Reeder, ed. Washington: The Liturgical Conference, 1981.

3. STORY

Arbuthnot, May Hill. *Arbuthnot Anthology of Children's Literature.* Glenview, Ill.: Scott, Foresman and Co., 1964.
_____. *Children and Books.* Glenview, Ill.: Scott, Foresman and Co., 1964.
Crossan, John Dominic. *The Dark Interval: Towards a Theology of Story.* Niles, Ill.: Argus Communications, 1975.
Dreyer, Sharon Spredemann. *The Book Finder.* Circle Pines, Minn.: American Guidance Service, Inc., 1977.
Eastman, Mary Huse. *Index to Fairy Tales, Myths and Legends.* Westwood, Mass.: F. W. Faxon Co., Inc., 1926.
Kirchner, Clara. *Behavior Patterns in Children's Books.* Washington: Catholic University of America Press, 1959.
Piveteau, Didier. "Biblical Pedagogies." In *Toward a Future for Religious Education,* J. M. Lee and Patrick Rooney, eds. Dayton: Pflaum Press, 1970. 93–114.
Sawyer, Ruth. *The Way of the Storyteller.* New York: Viking Press, Inc., 1962.
Shea, John. *Stories of God.* Chicago: The Thomas More Press, 1978.
Sutherland, Zena, ed. *Best in Children's Books.* Chicago: University of Chicago Press, 1973.

4. COMMON PRAYER — EUCHARIST

Aune, Michael B., and Roloff, Marvin L., eds. *Holy Communion Narrative for Children.* Minneapolis: Augsburg, 1978.
Freburger, William J. "Eucharistic Prayers for Children." *The Living Light* 12 (Fall 1975) 450–456.
Haas, James E. "A Modest Proposal for Celebrating Sacraments with Children." *The Living Light* 12 (Fall 1975) 457–460.
Holmes, Urban T. *Young Children and the Eucharist.* New York: Seabury Press, 1972.
Huck, Gabe. "The Directory Revisited." *Modern Liturgy* 4 (September–October 1977) 10.
Krosnicki, Thomas A. "The Directory for Masses with Children: A Commentary." *The Living Light* 11 (Summer 1974) 195–204.
Ling, Richard. "Commentary: Directory for Masses with Children." *Liturgy* 19 (April 1974) 20–22.
Matthews, Edward. *Celebrating Mass with Children.* New York: Paulist Press, 1978.
Sacred Congregation for Divine Worship. *Directory for Masses with Children.* Washington: United States Catholic Conference, 1973.
Thomson, Fred. *Celebrations for Children: The Complete Guide to Organizing and Celebrating Eucharistic Liturgies for Children.* West Mystic, Conn.: Twenty-Third Publications, 1978.

5. LITURGY — MORE THAN WORDS

Bishops' Committee on the Liturgy. *Eucharistic Prayers for Masses with Children and for Masses of Reconciliation.* Washington: United States Catholic Conference, 1975.
Bruce, Violet R., and Tooke, Jane. *Lord of the Dance: An Approach to Religious Education.* Elmsford, New York: Pergamon Press, Inc., 1966.
Collins, Mary. "Ritual Symbols: Something Human Between Us and God." *The Living Light* 12 (Fall 1975) 438–448.
DeSola, Carla. *The Spirit Moves: A Handbook of Dance and Prayer.* Washington: The Liturgical Conference, 1977.
Dubroillet, Jane. *Of Such Is the Kingdom of Heaven.* New York: Paulist Press, 1978.
Dubuisson, Odile. *Children, Crayons and Christ: Understanding the Religious Art of Children.* New York: Paulist Press, 1969.
Ferguson, Helen. *Bring on the Puppets.* Wilton, Conn.: Morehouse-Barlow, 1975.
Hubbard, Celia, ed. *Let's See No. 1: The Use and Misuse of Visual Arts in Religious Education.* New York: Paulist Press, 1966.
Hymnal for Young Christians. Los Angeles: F.E.L. Publications, 1968.
Jacquez-Dalcroze, Emile. *Rhythm, Music and Education.* Lombard, Ill.: Riverside Publishing Co., 1967.

Jeep, Elizabeth McMahon. *Classroom Creativity: An Idea Book for Religion Teachers.* New York: Seabury Press, 1977.

Kinghorn, Carol Jean, and Landry, Carey. *Celebrating Jesus.* Phoenix: North American Liturgy Resources, 1977.

Kussrow, V. "Fantasy, Imagination and Liturgy: The Grave-Merry Children of God at Play." *Liturgy* 24 (January-February 1979) 5-8, 27-29.

Meltz, Ken. "A Program for Affective Liturgy." In *Aesthetic Dimensions of Religious Education,* Gloria Durka and Joanmarie Smith, eds. New York: Paulist Press, 1979. 85-99.

Miller, Bob, and Miller, Margaret. "Children Listen with Their Whole Bodies." *Modern Liturgy* 4 (September-October 1977) 8-9.

Murphy, Jack, and Murphy, Arlene Wrigley. *Doing, Dance and Drama.* Notre Dame, Ind.: Ave Maria Press, 1980.

National Conference of Catholic Bishops. *To Teach as Jesus Did.* Washington: United States Catholic Conference, 1973.

O'Gorman, Dennis. *Scriptural Dramas for Children.* New York: Paulist Press, 1973-1976.

Ortegel, Adelaide. *A Dancing People.* West Lafayette, Ind.: The Center for Contemporary Celebration, 1976.

The Rites of the Catholic Church as Revised by the Second Vatican Council. New York: Pueblo Publishing Co., 1976.

Sacred Congregation for Divine Worship. *Directory for Masses with Children.* Washington: United States Catholic Conference, 1974.

_____. "Instruction on Masses for Special Groups." In *Vatican Council II.* Austin Flannery, ed. New York: Costello Publishing Co., 1975. 142-147.

Schreivogel, Paul. *The World of Art—The World of Youth: A Primer on the Use of Arts in Youth Ministry.* Minneapolis: Augsburg, 1968.

Seeger, Ruth Crawford, ed. *American Folk Songs for Children.* Garden City, N.Y.: Doubleday and Co., Inc., 1948.

Sharing the Light of Faith: National Catechetical Directory for Catholics of the United States. Washington: United States Catholic Conference, 1979.

Siks, Geraldine. *Creative Dramatics: An Art for Children.* New York: Harper and Row, 1958.

_____, ed. *Children's Literature for Dramatization: An Anthology.* New York: Harper and Row, 1964.

Taylor, Margaret Fisk. *Dramatic Dance with Children in Education and Worship.* Austin, Texas: Sharing Co., 1977.

_____. *A Time to Dance: Symbolic Movement in Worship.* Austin, Texas: Sharing Co., 1967.

Tuthill, Marge. *In the Image of God.* New York: Paulist Press, 1976.

Waddy, Lawrence. *Drama in Worship.* New York: Paulist Press, 1978.

Ward, Winifred. *Playmaking with Children.* Englewood Cliffs, N.J.: Appleton-Century-Crofts, 1957.

_____, ed. *Stories to Dramatize.* New Orleans: Anchorage Press, 1952.

Wise, Joe. *The Body at Liturgy.* Phoenix: North American Liturgy Resources, 1972.

6. SAMPLES

Haas, James, and Haas, Lynn. *Make a Joyful Noise.* Wilton, Conn.: Morehouse-Barlow, 1973.

_____. *Shout Hooray.* Wilton, Conn.: Morehouse-Barlow, 1973.

Huck, Gabe. *Major Feasts and Seasons.* Washington: The Liturgical Conference, 1975-1977.

Mossi, John P. *Modern Liturgy Handbook: A Study and Planning Guide for Worship.* New York: Paulist Press, 1976.